D1475534

Made in the USA
Columbia, SC
14 July 2021

41591537R00075

"The miracles recorded in this book are gloriously amazing. As you read its pages, you will be motivated to believe God for greater things in your life and ministry. I am grateful for Brent's selfless passion for the advancement of Christ's kingdom. I am also grateful for his personal friendship. He and Michelle are truly chosen of God for the mission in which they are engaged."

PAUL RUSSELL
Lead Pastor, Christ Family Church, Cypress, TX

"This book was a breath of fresh air and a page turner. When I began to read, I could not stop. I craved the rest of the story. I believe this type of book is very much needed in the body of Christ. It is my belief that Christians in the American culture are fearful of the supernatural. Many in the church today just do not believe in miracles. Only when people witness a miracle with their own eyes do they then believe. The longer I live, I believe that 'Nothing is impossible with God.' I have witnessed and experienced His hand at work in ways that were supernatural, so it is important that believers read about what God is doing in the world today. This type of book is a must read for anyone who is interested in or doing any type of Christian ministry."

PAUL GILMORE
President, Light for Living, Clinton, MS

"In 1999, Brent Knapton and I, along with three others, traveled to Manipur, India, as he describes in Chapter 7. Brent clearly documents the amazing ways that God opened doors into territories where Westerners were not previously allowed. This and many other accounts in this book demonstrate the power and glory of God. *Testimonies of Grace* illustrates the fact that God is able to use any believer who follows as God leads. As Brent reminds us, our lives can be life-giving, like the Sea of Galilee, rather than poisonous, like the Dead Sea, which has no outlet. *Testimonies of Grace* illustrates to the reader what God can do through each of us."

DR. PAUL RAINS
Christ In You Ministries, Ellington, MO

"I met Brent when he was in the youth group at Bedford Methodist and I was a summer youth intern. Later, as a Methodist pastor, I had the privilege to officiate Brent and Michelle's wedding. This power couple has always been obedient to God's calling in their lives, and I have loved hearing the testimonies of God's mighty power working in them as missionaries. This book is so encouraging and exciting that I could not put it down until I read it cover to cover! I was inspired to see God's miraculous, redemptive works lived out in such a glorious way! *Testimonies of Grace* will motivate you to obediently follow God and allow Him to impact the world for His glory."

REV. MIKE MAYHUGH
First United Methodist, Henderson, TX

"I have known Brent for over ten years as part of a men's group, Brothers Helping Others. *Testimonies of Grace* is a story of how Brent has allowed God to use him to reach many lost souls. I have heard all these stories from Brent over the years, so it is a blessing to have access to all of them in print. I know Brent's journey has inspired me in my journey and will no doubt inspire many others in their journey to become more Christ-like and share the Good News with others."

RICK SIMS
Brothers Helping Others, Cypress, TX

"I was so blessed and encouraged to go through *Testimonies of Grace*. It has wonderful testimonies of how God is working and transforming people in so many parts of the world. Please take time to read this book prayerfully. It will encourage you to love and serve God faithfully, which will definitely have eternal value."

REV. DR. T. N. LOTHA JR.
Principal, Eastern Bible College and
President, Nagaland National Christian Council,
Nagaland, INDIA

"What an honor for me to meet Rev. Brent in May, 1998, in Kathmandu, Nepal, when I was just graduating from Kathmandu Theological Seminary. As we shared Christ together in West Nepal, I felt in my heart a spiritual fellowship, and his mentoring shaped and equipped me in the ministry where I am today, 22 years later. I see in Rev. Brent the burning passion for the Gospel and missions and for equipping and uplifting young leaders around the world. When I heard Rev. Brent had written a book, I knew it would be not just an ordinary book but an inspiring life-testimony of his personal reflections on walking with Christ. Not everyone is called to go to the mission field, but this book can give them a vision for it. I am extremely excited that *Testimonies of Grace* will be a resource for many missionaries, Christian leaders, and church planters whose hearts beat for missions."

REV. NANDA KUMAR GURUNG
Vice President, National Christian Council of India and
President, North-East India, National Christian Council of India
West Bengal, INDIA

"*Testimonies of Grace* is a wonderful journey through one man's experiences in faith and his obedience to share the Word of God wherever he is sent. Brent shares very honest accounts of his thoughts and feelings of encounters with the Lord, the places and experiences he had on mission trips, and his desire to share the Gospel to the unreached. With its straightforward approach, this book is a great read for anyone who has a heart to serve the Lord, whether to motivate a lay person in their local congregation or to encourage a missionary on the field."

ROGIE GEORGE
Brother in Christ, Stafford, TX

"I met Brent for the first time through my close brother in Lord, Rev. Nandu Gurung. During our week together, I sensed, without a shadow of a doubt, that Brent was a man of passion, commitment, and mission. Later, I came to know he was a LIVE School Ambassador for India. After being trained, I decided to start a LIVE School in Dalsingpara, near the border of Bhutan for many leaders and believers. Brent has been a very encouraging, supportive, and concerned leader. As we have continued to meet and pray online, it has been my joy to know him better. What a gripping way to begin a glorious journey and a book: "Brent Knapton hears from God." His divine call, absolute obedience, and undivided engagement in missions will surely move the heart, challenge the mind, and energize the feet of every reader, leader, and believer for the Great Mission to which God has called us. As you read, let God's rivers become waterfalls in and through you as well."

REV. SATISH CHETTRI
Co-founder and Sr. Pastor, Delhi Nepali Christian Fellowship,
New Delhi, INDIA

TESTIMONIES OF GRACE

When Rivers Become Waterfalls

BRENT KNAPTON

To learn more or contact Brent, visit:
BRENTKNAPTON.COM

Transcribed by Michelle Knapton.
Illustration on page 96 by Diana Marino:
instagram.com/dianmmari
Designed and edited by Eric Elder:
ericelder.com

ISBN: 9798517465269

Table of Contents

Thank you, Michelle, for giving me grace
to fulfill God's calling on our lives.

"The women at home divide the spoil."
Psalm 68:12b (ESV)

Eric Elder, with Michelle and Brent Knapton, on a writing retreat to create this book, May, 2021.

Foreword – Hearing from God
by Eric Elder
Editor, Friend, and Founder of The Ranch

Brent Knapton hears from God. And not just for himself, but for many others, including me. I can say that God has spoken to me through Brent more than any other person.

How has this affected me? It's given me confidence to move forward in what God has called me to do. It's given me wisdom to know which way to turn at crucial junctions in my life. And it's given me unfathomable comfort to know that God is with me when facing the most difficult situations.

I was at Brent and Michelle's house when God spoke clearly to me to quit my secular job of ten years and go into full-time ministry, which I did within hours of leaving their house. That was over 25 years ago, and I've never looked back.

I was with Brent at a men's retreat in Texas when God said He would speak very specifically to each of the twenty-some men who were gathered that night through a talk I was giving. At one point in my talk, Brent held up his hand to say that it was done – that God had spoken to each one. I stopped talking immediately and one by one, with no prompting from either of us, each man at the retreat came up to me personally in the hours that followed to tell me how God had spoken to them very specifically about something personal in their lives.

I was on the phone with Brent when God gave him a picture in his mind of a ranch where God wanted me to live. Brent sketched out the picture, wrote "The Ranch" on the top, and faxed it to me addressed to Pastor Eric Elder. The picture featured a creek and a fence, trees and a sunset, obstacles to overcome and a lone tree in the foreground casting its shadow on the creek. I wasn't a pastor at the time, and I wasn't planning on moving! But one year later, to the day, I was living at that very spot, a property which neither of us had ever seen before nor heard about — and I was hired and ordained as a pastor! I went on to found a ministry which I run to this day called "The Ranch" at www.theranch.org.

So when I say that Brent hears from God and that what he hears is not only for himself but for others, too, I say it wholeheartedly.

I'd also like to say a word about Michelle. Some people are worriers and some people are warriors. Michelle is a warrior — a prayer warrior! She has supported Brent both by his side and from afar, as much a part of the team in either location. If you ever need prayer or a word of encouragement, go to Michelle!

As you read through the stories that follow, you'll see how God has touched people all over the world through Brent and Michelle — through their tenderhearted listening for God's still, small voice and their obedience to do whatever God says to do, no matter how impossible it might seem.

I am 100% confident that if *you* want to hear from God, and you're willing to listen for His still, small voice, *you'll* hear Him speak to you through the pages of this book, too. Like the apostle John, Brent wrote these stories for one reason alone: *"that you may believe that Jesus is the Christ, the Son of God; and that by believing you may have life in His name" (John 20:31).*

Eric Elder

A majestic waterfall on the border of China and Vietnam.

I. Introduction – Waterfalls of Grace

Testimonies of Grace contains some of my personal stories giving God glory. It is a book about God not only showing up but showing off. He pours out, reveals, manifests, and delivers His grace upon me and others despite our weaknesses, failures, sinfulness, and sometimes willful disobedience.

Grace is more than undeserved favor. It is the continual outpouring of gifts and blessings and the empowering to do God's will. I don't have the strength or endurance or capability to follow God every day of my life, but God, in His infinite wisdom and great grace, encourages, equips, enthuses, and energizes me to accomplish His will, even when I am not fully cooperating with Him. God gets His will done in spite of me.

Grace is not however, a license to sin. This is an immature and very dangerous, compromising attitude to have. Christians must deny themselves, not indulge themselves. Christians must crucify and starve the lusts of the carnal nature and not feed them to where they grow. The apostle Paul said it best:

Romans 6:1-2 (ESV)

"What shall we say then? Are we to continue in sin that grace may abound? By no means! How can we who died to sin still live in it?"

Galatians 5:24 (ESV)

"And those who belong to Christ Jesus have crucified the flesh with its passions and desires."

So I have a choice. I can surrender and follow God's will, God's plans, and God's ways and enjoy the journey with peace and joy in my heart, or I can resist selfishly and then become convicted because God, even in my falling back into sinfulness, is still gracious to me. Remember, this is no excuse to allow sinful behavior to control your life. A mature person is motivated by God's love and grace and forgiveness to not sin because we are reminded of the great value of His sacrificial gift given to us who do not deserve it and can never repay it. If we trample upon the grace of God, we will not go undisciplined, for God chastises every child He loves (see Hebrews 12:6). Nonetheless, the grace of God is abundant. It is overwhelming. It is miraculous. It is free-flowing. It is what happens when a river becomes a waterfall!

A river flows across flat terrain until it reaches a transition point, then it drops vertically as a mighty torrent of beauty and powerful free-falling energy. A waterfall is accelerated by the force of gravity to the earth from a significant height, displaying power and majesty and glory and beauty as it continuously flows. The same waterfall that cleanses us also empowers us. You can put a waterwheel under a waterfall to convert power into electricity which can light up an entire community. So God places us, at times, under His waterfall of grace to shine the light of His goodness and power and glory to those living in darkness.

So we either stand under the waterfall and are cleansed and empowered or we choose to walk in the wilderness of thirst and barrenness. Your choice.

God's grace is the water. All the drops of the water combined in the right quantity at the right time. If you need one drop or ten drops, the greater the flow of grace, the greater the power, the greater the ministry. God doesn't always saturate me with the waterfall. A single drop can have significant impact as well! It not only touches me, it touches others.

John 4:14
"...but whoever drinks of the water that I will give him shall never be thirsty; but the water that I will give him will become in him a fountain of water springing up to eternal life."

John 7:38
"The one who believes in Me, as the Scripture said, 'From his innermost being will flow rivers of living water.' "

So the flow of grace leads to powerful testimonies in our lives. The greatest flow of God's Grace occurred at Calvary, and if you are a Christian you have a personal testimony of how God chose you and how you responded to Him. This book contains my salvation experience and a select few, true testimonies of how God has worked through my life and teammates to touch others.

Revelation 12:11
"And they overcame him because of the blood of the Lamb and because of the word of their testimony, and they did not love their life even when faced with death."

One of the most amazing testimonies recorded in the New Testament is when Jesus walked to His disciples on water when they were experiencing a huge storm in their lives (see Matthew 14:25-33). Jesus called to Peter, "Come!" and he responded to the call and walked on water. It was God's grace that sustained him. Faith got him over the edge of the boat, grace sustained him over the water, and doubt sunk him under when he took His eyes off of Jesus and looked at the overwhelming circumstances surrounding him.

We respond in faith, but we're sustained by grace, so long as we maintain our focus on Christ and don't allow the world around us to pull us under. I have often wondered if Peter shared his "water-walking testimony" very often in the years that followed? If he had made it all the way to Jesus, I think he would have, but because he sank, I think he perhaps refrained from sharing the story too often or publicly at all. In the same way, I have been reluctant to write about these testimonies because I do not want people to elevate me or think I am doing it for self-serving motives. I honestly can share with you that I am writing this book out of obedience to the Lord and praying that it rekindles a sense of wonder and amazement at what God can do in and through the lives of ordinary believers, *"common, uneducated,"* people as Peter and John were described in Acts 4:13. Now in no way am I disparaging Christian education or studying to *"show oneself approved."* This is a calling and much needed pursuit in our day and time as the Christian world view is under attack and being opposed by socialism and anti-Christian neo-paganism to name a few. God had a different route for me to take, quite unorthodox and unique.

My message is simple: If God can pour out His grace upon me, He can pour it out upon you, also. Don't be afraid to step out in faith and obey God's call to whatever He is calling you to be and become. He will take care of the "doing" part; you make sure you are "becoming" the follower of Christ He wants you to be.

To put it even simpler: "Follow Jesus"!

A dramatic dream prompted Brent's mom to share Christ's love and peace with him at age nine.

II. Salvation at an early age (1976)

"For by grace you have been saved through faith; and this is not of yourselves, it is the gift of God; not a result of works, so that no one may boast."
Ephesians 2:8-9

The night of April 17th, 1976, is one that I will never forget. I woke up from a dream which was causing me to weep in anguish over what I saw. In the dream, it was as if I had jumped out of a plane with a parachute, and I was descending through the air. As I was falling, the atmosphere around me became darker and darker, as if I was in a dark rain cloud. I then began to hear a multitude of voices crying in torment. I woke up before I approached the bottom of whatever I was falling into and did not see any more.

My mother, Sandra Knapton, woke up from my crying out and came into the room to see what was the matter. I described to her my dream and she shared with me that I must have been dreaming about what it was like to be separated from God. Even though I was only nine years old, I had an acute awareness of my sinfulness and mortality. My mom went on to tell me that God had sent Jesus into the world to be our savior, and because of His death on the cross and His resurrection from the dead, He was able to remove our sin and give us a new life.

At that moment, I was very eager to ask Jesus to save me. When I did, I immediately sensed an overwhelming peace surrounding me and to this day I have had a strong awareness of God's presence with me in my life. It was as if Jesus had reached down with His mighty hand and grabbed my parachute and kept me from falling into the dark abyss.

I did not know many Bible verses at that time, but I knew God loved me and was rescuing me from a life of selfishness to surrender my life in selflessness to Him.

That night I lost my sinful life, but I received God's righteous life. I have, despite trials and negative circumstances in life, always had an abiding sense of security and assurance of God's love not just for me but for all people. This single event has been the strongest motivator for me to share the great gospel of Jesus Christ with people I meet and those to whom God has sent me.

2 Corinthians 5:16-21 (ESV)

"From now on, therefore we regard no one according to the flesh.

"Even though we once regarded Christ according to the flesh, we regard Him thus no longer. Therefore if anyone is in Christ, he is a new creation. The old has passed away; behold, the new has come. All this is from God, who through Christ reconciled us to Himself and gave us the ministry of reconciliation; that is, in Christ God was reconciling the world to Himself, not counting their trespasses against them and entrusting to us the message of reconciliation.

"Therefore, we are ambassadors for Christ, God making His appeal through us. We implore you on behalf of Christ, be reconciled to God.

"For our sake He was made sin who knew no sin, so that in Him we might become the righteousness of God."

An ambassador has been given the authority to represent the country from which he or she has been sent. An ambassador lives in a foreign country representing one's home country. The great grace of God gives us the ministry of reconciliation whereby we tell the people living in the foreign country (i.e. the kingdom of this world) how it is to live in the home country, i.e. the kingdom of God. All cultures and ethnicities are welcome to enter and live in the home country regardless of their economic, social or cultural status. All that is required to make the transition is faith in Jesus Christ.

Brent led his first mission trip at age 21 to Haiti in 1987.

Back row: Susan Jackson, Shauna Peterson Kimberly Worley, Kelly Earley, Jill Sharples, Patricia Mumme, Stephanie Bishop, Jennifer Burford, YWAM missionaries. Front row: YWAM missionary, Mike Clothier, Mike Mason, Drew Starnes, Jace Beasley, Brent Knapton, Jon Pignatelli, Mark Dostert, Brian Sellers, Terry Snow.

III. Led first mission trip to Haiti (1987)

"Therefore let's approach the throne of grace with confidence, so that we may receive mercy and find grace for help at the time of our need."
Hebrews 4:16

The summer before my junior year at Rice University, I joined some of the youth from Bedford Methodist with youth pastor Mark Morrow on a mission trip to England. Little did I know that my girlfriend at the time Michelle Stearns, who also went on the trip, would later become my wife.

The next summer, Mark asked me to lead the summer mission trip because he needed to coordinate activities for the large majority of the youth who were out of school. I was excited and honored for being given this responsibility, so I prayed earnestly and sensed God put the nation of Haiti on my heart.

I made contact with the leader of a Youth With a Mission (YWAM) team in Haiti named Terry Snow. He welcomed a group from our church for two weeks to help build a church in the mountains north of Port Au Prince.

God raised up twenty team members, and we rented a bus and drove from Bedford, Texas, to Jacksonville, Florida. We boarded the Mercy Ship *Good Samaritan* and sailed two days before arriving in Haiti. The weather was calm, but many of the team suffered seasickness as a result of the constant motion of the waves.

I will never forget the scene as our ship pulled in to dock at the port. Dozens of Haitians came up along the boat in small canoes begging for money or attempting to sell us handcrafts. When we disembarked down the gangplank onto Haitian soil, we were totally inundated by more Haitians begging and trying to sell us their wares. We were also greeted by the YWAM leaders who escorted us to their jeep and truck and drove us up the mountain to the village of Ferrier where the church was going to be built.

We had a wonderful first week working on the church building. We took a day off to rest, and we drove down to sightsee and shop in the Port Au Prince market. On the way down, one of our team members, Kelly Earley, began to complain of abdominal pain, and Terry and I took Kelly to the Mercy Ship to see the onboard nurse. As Terry and I were sitting in the jeep waiting, an elderly Haitian man wearing a white shirt and pants came up to me holding a book and pointing to Ephesians chapter 6. He didn't say a word. He then closed his Bible and walked off into the crowd and disappeared.

At that moment, the nurse brought Kelly off the ship and said an ultrasound had shown she had an ovarian cyst and needed to be taken to a hospital immediately. Terry and I drove Kelly to the nearest hospital where the doctors asked permission to operate immediately on Kelly. I called her father and asked for his consent for the surgery, but he refused and instructed me to put her on the next available flight back home to Texas.

While Kelly was being evaluated by doctors in the hospital, Terry and I were in the waiting room asking the Lord to give us wisdom and to heal Kelly. I shared with

Terry that it was very encouraging that the Haitian man had shown me Ephesians 6 in his Bible, which talks about the power of prayer. Terry looked at me and said, "What man?"

I said, "Didn't you see the man holding the Bible and pointing to Ephesians chapter 6?"

Terry began to weep as he told me that God had told him the same verses to pray and stand in the gap for the nation of Haiti when He called him to be a missionary. I then called the airline and booked a one-way ticket for Kelly, but I had to use the credit card of one of the team members because I didn't have enough funds to purchase the ticket.

We drove to the airport and the agent was not going to let her fly because her passport was not stamped. This was because we initially arrived by boat, not airplane, and the immigration cleared our cargo but did not require a stamp in our passports. I appealed to the airline representative that Kelly was in a great deal of discomfort and her family was waiting for her back in the U.S. and she graciously allowed Kelly to board the plane without a stamp in her passport.

We then drove back to the village of Ferrier where we showed the *Jesus* film that night and many accepted Christ as their savior.

The next week, we finished building the church and returned back to the ship to make our way home. I was amazed to hear the news that when Kelly was taken to a local hospital in Texas, the doctors could find no traces of the cyst on her ovaries! God had apparently healed her on the airline flight! It is really true where the scripture says:

Acts 4:30 (ESV)

"And now, Lord, look upon their threats and grant to your servants to continue to speak with all boldness, while You stretch out Your hand to heal and signs and wonders are performed through Your holy servant, Jesus."

Malachi 4:2 (ESV)

"But for you who fear my name, the sun of righteousness shall rise with healing in its wings. You shall go out like calves leaping from the stall."

God was indeed gracious to take a college student leading a bunch of teenagers, and despite our inexperience and limited resources, God used us to bring people to meet Christ and build a place to worship and be discipled. Although Kelly's sickness was an attack from the enemy to try to prevent the showing of the *Jesus* film, God prevailed in every way and He is to be praised. I often wonder if the man who came up to the jeep was an angel for several reasons:

1. He came up at the exact right moment to bring a word of encouragement to me.
2. Terry was sitting right next to me in an open jeep and did not see him.
3. He had a Bible at a time when 87 percent of elderly Haitians were illiterate and not Christian.
4. He didn't beg for money or sell me anything like most Haitians in the Port location.
5. He never spoke or uttered a word. He just pointed with his finger to a specific verse and chapter in the Bible.
6. The appearance of his hair and clothing was pure white. It is something I will never forget!

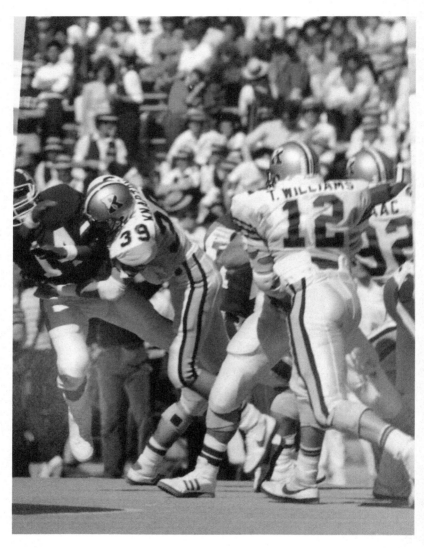

Brent Knapton (#39), playing safety for Rice University in 1987, sacking Kevin Murray (#14), future father of 2018 Heisman Trophy winner, Kyler Murray.

IV. Ministry at Rice University (1984 – 1989)

"And He has said to me, 'My grace is sufficient for you, for power is perfected in weakness.' Most gladly, therefore, I will rather boast about my weaknesses, so that the power of Christ may dwell in me."
2 Corinthians 12:9

a. Voddie Baucham - "Called to Preach"

My friend and football teammate Max Moss and I were conducting Fellowship of Christian Athletes (FCA) meetings weekly on the campus of Rice University in 1987.

Through the faculty sponsorship of Julie Griswold (Student Athlete Academic Advisor), Max and I re-established an FCA chapter at Rice which had not had one in over a decade. A handful of athletes would faithfully attend the meetings, and Max and I would trade off leading the discussions around a verse of Scripture. Because we were a newly formed chapter of FCA at Rice, we were laying a foundation upon which God could build.

One day, the Houston regional director of FCA asked us to bring a group of athletes to a retreat setting to join other university and high school athletes in a conference-style gathering for a weekend of fellowship and inspirational messages. As I began to pray about this opportunity, I sensed the Lord very specifically commanding me to pray 30 minutes a day for 30 days for 30 athletes to go on the retreat. (When I share this testimony, I always tell people not to copy this particular prayer mandate but to always seek the Lord for His will in their particular situation. After I share this story, I think you will have a better understanding about why the Lord was so specific to require us to pray for 30 athletes.)

In obedience, Max and I set a specific time after lunch each day and kept a notepad of athletes we would invite to the retreat, and we daily updated this list at each prayer time. By faith, we rented three vans which would hold ten people each. When Friday finally came for us to drive from Houston to Central Texas for the retreat, Max and I showed up at the football stadium at 3 pm and were delighted to see several athletes ready to go with an overall count of 29. I immediately had a sense of urgency and spontaneity. I thought to myself, "God, you have promised that if we prayed, you would bring 30 athletes on this trip, and Max and I were obedient to do what You said to do!" I told Max, "Here, hold my Bible," and jumped in my car and drove through the Rice campus praying for one more athlete to join our retreat. I left the others and went to look for the "30th wandering sheep."

I reached a stop sign, and as I sat there, lo and behold I saw a football player, Voddie Baucham, walking across the street to class. I motioned for him to come over. I asked him to go to the retreat, but he said he needed to go to class instead, and besides, he would have no clothes for the whole weekend. I told him that we had players who could loan him clothes and to skip class because this was more important to him. How we would get him clothing that would fit him was indeed a stretch (pun intended), because Voddie was one of the largest players on the team. He reluctantly got in the car and started back with me to the football stadium where 28 guys were waiting patiently. Then the 30 of us drove to the retreat in the vans.

That night, the keynote speaker delivered a message that impacted Voddie to the point that he knelt on the floor for several minutes then stood up and declared, "God has called me to preach!" To say that I was somewhat in shock was an understatement. I asked Voddie if he had a Bible, and he said "No."

I then gave him my Bible and told him, "You better read this if you are going to preach." He stayed up the whole night reading the entire New Testament. The next day he was filled with joy and couldn't wait to return to Rice to start exercising his calling.

When we got back to campus he openly shared about his experience and began telling students about what God had done in his life. Many students were drawn to Voddie because of the authority by which he spoke and the transformation that was taking place in his life. I asked Voddie to start speaking each week at the FCA meetings, and the attendance grew from an average of 20 athletes to over 200, mostly students!

Not long after this, Voddie decided to stop playing football and transfer to Houston Baptist University (HBU) where he could be trained in theology and how to preach. I fully supported this decision and soon thereafter was called into my head football coach's office, where he demanded an explanation of why Voddie was leaving the team. Our coach blamed me for Voddie quitting the team and demanded I try to change his mind because he was a starter on both offense (tight end) and defense (linebacker) and was destined to be drafted into the NFL. I took great joy in telling my coach that I would never stand in the way of God calling someone to prepare for full-time ministry, and I refused to talk to Voddie about him reconsidering his decision.

I left that meeting feeling a sense of conviction but also despair. I told one of my teammates, Scott Reeves, that we would not win a game in our upcoming season. Sure enough, we went 0-11 in one of the most disappointing seasons in Rice's history. Rice University lost a great football player, but the Church of Jesus Christ gained a great apologist, author, and educator! I had no idea at the time how God might use him in the future, but I was sure he was supposed to be on the retreat that weekend. And what a blessing to have Voddie preach at my own ordination service just three years later.

Acts 9: 10 –12, 15 (NKJV)

"Now there was a certain disciple at Damascus named Ananias; and to him the Lord said in a vision, 'Ananias.' And he said, 'here I am, Lord,' So the Lord said to him, 'Arise and go to the street called Straight, and inquire at the house of Judas for one called Saul of Tarsus, for behold, he is praying. And in a vision he had seen a man named Ananias coming in and putting his hand on him, so that he might receive his sight.' … The Lord said to him, 'Go, for he is a chosen vessel of Mine to bear My name before Gentiles, kings, and the children of Israel.' "

Because of the significant growth of our weekly FCA meetings, several things happened. First, I saw the need to start a separate Bible study to begin to disciple some of the athletes who were just starting their new life in Christ. Not only did we have football players in this group, but God brought Jeffery Cranford from the golf team, now the Founding Pastor of Church at the Red Door in Palm Springs, CA, and Director of Links Players and Rodney Burton from the tennis team, now doing ministry and living in Australia with his wife Fiona and family.

I have often reflected back on those days at Rice and wondered what if I had accepted a football scholarship to Stanford instead of Rice? What if Max and I had not completed our prayer mandate and had been satisfied with only 29 athletes going on the retreat? What if I arrived at the stop sign ten seconds later and had not seen Voddie cross my path? What if Voddie had not agreed to get in my car and had gone to his class instead?

I used to think that God would have used someone else to get Voddie to a different Christian meeting somewhere else at some other time. But the truth of the matter is that God, in His infinite wisdom and abundant grace, led me to choose Rice over Stanford. God gave Max and me the grace to faithfully pray and be motivated to go and seek one more athlete to fulfill His will. God timed the departure time of our trip, the distance I would drive onto the campus, the time of Voddie's class, and the route he would take that day to coincide at the exact right moment (a "Kairos" moment – the fullness of time when divine grace intersects with human surrender to accomplish God's will) for His will to be done "on earth as it is in heaven." God, by His grace, was working in Voddie's heart to call him to something greater than a degree from Rice or a position in the NFL. Yes, there was NO WAY Voddie and I would *not* have met on that Friday afternoon – it was God's divine providence and will for it to happen... and it did!

Ephesians 2:10 (NKJV)
"For we are His workmanship, created in Christ Jesus for good works, which God prepared beforehand that we should walk in them."

b. God says, "That's not what I have for you."

After studying five long years and about to receive two degrees in Mechanical Engineering and Religious Studies from Rice University, I decided I wanted to attend Fuller Seminary in California. I filled out the application and requested and received reference letters from two professors, and I was not interviewing with any corporations on campus for an engineering job after graduation. I had my heart set on finally being trained in ministry, and I was certain I would be accepted based on the credentials I was submitting.

I will never forget the day I went to mail my application package, filled with excitement and anticipation as I was about to drop it in the opening, and God clearly admonished me, saying, **"That is not what I have for you."** I was stunned, shocked, and amazed, along with severely disappointed. I could not understand why God would prohibit me from pursuing my dream? I knew in that moment that if I dropped the application in the mailbox, I would be disobedient.

Wisely, I restrained myself, yet immaturely became angry with God because He was preventing me from doing what I wanted to do. I felt all alone and didn't know what to do next. I wasn't inclined to pray, so I walked slowly back to my car and drove home. The next day, I went to the student center and asked if they had any more corporations interviewing on campus. There was only one, so I signed up for an interview the following day. Graciously, I was offered a job and took it because it was the only option I had.

That summer I went home and proposed to my girl-friend of seven years, Michelle Stearns. We set a wedding date of June 16th, 1990, and had a wonderful yearlong engagement where we spent many hours discussing and planning our wedding ceremony, the invitation list, what items we wanted to put on our shopping list, and where we would spend our honeymoon. After our wedding, of-ficiated by Rev. Mike Mayhugh, we departed to Brecken-ridge, Colorado, on Lake Dillon, enjoying our time there sightseeing, white water rafting, and hiking.

After our wonderful getaway, we returned to our apartment in west Houston, and I continued to work at Stone & Webster Corporation and Michelle taught kindergarten at Bear Creek Elementary. We continued to attend Grace Covenant church, pastored by Mark Mc-Climens and his wife Pat. Three years after our wedding, Michelle was pregnant with the first of our four sons, Luke. He was born October 12, 1993, and we moved into our first house in the Fairfield subdivision in Cypress, west of Houston. We visited Fairfield Baptist church, which was meeting in the recreation center. We met dear life-long friends: Max and Lisa Moss, Bill and Kim Roberts, Bill and Mary Slattery, and Rick and Linda Jones. We soon became charter members being discipled by pas-tor Jim Daniel and his wife Carla, now leaders of Still Wa-ters Renewal, a counseling ministry to pastors, missionar-ies, and church leaders.

I had a plan that seemed right to me, but thankfully, God showed me that He had other plans.

Acts 4:13 (ESV)

"Now when they saw the boldness of Peter and John, and per-ceived that they were uneducated, common men, they were aston-ished. And they recognized that they had been with Jesus."

God inspired Brent about both a vision and provision through a common form.

V. The Call (1995)

"But when He who had set me apart even from my mother's womb and called me through His grace..."
Galatians 1:15

I had been working for five years at Stone & Webster designing fired heaters, heat transfer equipment, and utility piping systems when God spoke to me a second time and said, **"Lay your career down at my altar."** All the same feelings of doubt, frustration, and confusion from a few years earlier came back as I contemplated, "What could this mean?"

I had wanted to go to Bible College as a teenager and seminary after college, but now God wanted me to serve Him in ministry with no training, a one-year-old son, and $600 in the bank. I enjoyed my job and had responsibilities to take care of my wife and son, so why was God wanting me to resign from my job at that moment in a most inopportune time?

For several months, I wrestled with the Lord but to no avail. I wore down, becoming tired and fatigued.

One day at work, I called Michelle at home and shared with her what God was leading me to do. I went into my boss's office, Mrinal Chaudhary, and informed him of my decision to resign. He was curious to know what I would be doing, and I honestly could not answer his question. I sensed God was calling me to some sort of ministry position, but I had no clue what it was going to entail. He immediately told me how impressed he was with Mother

Teresa from his home country of India, and he got out his checkbook and gave me the first gift towards ministry. Little did I know that I would travel to India more than eighteen times in the coming years. This conversation prompted me to ask the Lord what I should tell people in the next two weeks about what I was doing. I thought they would either think I was a fool or a hero for doing what I intended, but I felt like neither. I asked the Lord what I should tell people who asked me, "What are you doing?"

The Lord said softly and reassuringly, **"Tell them about Me."** It was as if a light went off in my mind, and I saw how self-centered and self-protecting I was in wanting an answer to tell people for my own sake. I repented and committed to share boldly with anyone who asked about why I was resigning.

Each day, fewer and fewer people came to my office as word spread I was sharing the Gospel with everybody who stopped by to talk to me. On the last day of my employment, I was approached by a lady at the copy machine. She heard I was telling people about Jesus and wanted to know more. She accepted Christ as her savior right there! With a great sense of excitement and joy, I left the building knowing I had at least impacted one individual for eternity.

The Monday morning after I resigned, I was at home, crying, and praying to the Lord, feeling sadness and loss and honestly regret at what I had done. Just then the phone rang. I answered it to hear a man named Robert asking me if I was available to preach at his church the next Sunday morning. I was confused because I did not know this individual or the church. As I asked him questions, another call came in and I asked Robert to hold as I accepted the other call…literally.

It was Cathy who said, "Hello, is Brent Knapton there?"

I said, "Yes, this is he."

Cathy said, "You don't know me, but I work at Stone & Webster and my name is Cathy. I was at the copy machine when you shared with the lady. I felt convicted because I haven't been to church for years. I then determined to go back to Greenvine Baptist Church with my husband that Sunday. Last Sunday, we rededicated our lives to the Lord. I mentioned your name to one of the leaders at the church that day as we do not have a pastor at the moment. I gave them your name and number. I hope you don't mind."

I said, "I am talking to Robert on the other line, and I will commit to preach at your church this coming Sunday."

Now in tears, Cathy said, "Oh, I prayed that God would use me!"

I said, "Yes, Cathy, God has used you. Thank you for sharing my name with your church leadership!"

For the next three months, I preached every Sunday morning. I stayed with a family every Sunday for those three months, driving to their church to preach in the morning, staying for lunch, then preaching again in the evening, then drove back home to Houston. God was teaching me how to study His word and prepare and deliver sermons, which was a greater responsibility than just leading small group studies, which I had done in the past.

Each week that passed, I began to sense that I wasn't called to be a preacher or a pastor, but rather to go and share Christ with people who had never heard the gospel. I shared our situation with Jim Daniel, my pastor at Fairfield Baptist Church, and he committed to pray for us every day and introduced me to a medical doctor who was on staff with Global Mission Fellowship.

I had lunch with him, and he invited me to go on a mission trip to Puerta Ordaz and San Feliz, Venezuela. The team was leaving in two weeks, so I had very little time to raise funds and get prepared. We arrived on a Saturday, and that night our team leader started having heart palpitations. We had to call an ambulance to rush him to the hospital for emergency care. He asked me to preach the Sunday message at the host church prior to the next week of evangelistic outreaches in a community called Coreocho.

The elderly, senior pastor preached at the early service in Spanish because he could not speak English. I was designated to preach at the late service in English with an interpreter. As I was sitting on the second row, I sensed from the Holy Spirit not to preach from the pulpit, but to stand near the front row of the church and deliver the message. I knew this would not be well received by the pastor, so I planned to talk to the pastor's interpreter after the early service message was concluded. But before I had a chance to talk to him, he exited out the back door. I was quite dismayed and asked the man sitting next to me, "Was the interpreter coming back for the second service?"

The man replied, "No, he goes down the street to our sister church and interprets there during the second service." So I asked if the man who was the interpreter for the second service was there.

He said, "I am."

I was overjoyed at this news and proceeded to explain to him that I needed to tell the senior pastor about God leading me to speak on the floor of the church and not the platform. But before I could talk to him, the senior pastor introduced me as the speaker and then sat down in the front row.

I stood with the interpreter on the floor next to him, and before I could speak a word, he stood back up and grabbed my arm and attempted to escort me up the steps to the pulpit. I asked my interpreter to explain to the pastor why I was not going to speak from the pulpit, and he reluctantly sat down.

I preached a message about God's love revealed in His son Jesus, that He provides forgiveness for our sins, and does not count our trespasses against us. I invited anyone who wanted to accept Christ as their savior, and three people did. Two were a Muslim couple who had just moved to Venezuela and had just heard the gospel for the first time. The third person was the senior pastor's estranged daughter, who had left the church in rebellion years before and, like the prodigal son, returned that morning curious to meet the team members from the United States.

Upon hearing the message, her heart was touched and she wanted to receive God's love and forgiveness. She heard the message from God's heart to her heart, speaking to her on her level, not from an authoritative figure in the pulpit. It was as if God put me close to her to speak His message personally to her. The whole church gathered around the pastor and his daughter as they embraced, reconciled, and reunited in the presence of God and the entire church.

Soon after returning from this mission trip, God prompted me to open the drawer of my filing cabinet and asked, **"What do you see?"**

I saw a the cover sheet of my tax return that said, "Form 1040."

God said, **"Just as this form reimburses funds owed to individuals back from the government, I am calling you to the 10/40 Window, and I will provide the funds for that which I'm calling you to do."**

The 10/40 Window is a region of the world stretching from North Africa across the Middle East and through India to Southeast Asia, between 10 degrees and 40 degrees above the equator. This area contains the largest concentration of people who have never heard the gospel of Jesus Christ.

"What about my credibility?" I asked.

"I AM the God of the incredible," God replied!

In a step of faith and obedience, I founded a non-profit mission organization called Window of Opportunity under the financial and spiritual oversight of Light for Living, founded by the late Charles Gilmore, now led by his sons, Paul and Bob Gilmore.

We brought on medical and volunteer staff to support our vision of hosting medical clinics during the days and evangelistic services in the evenings across the 10/40 Window in the countries of South Korea, Cambodia (3x), Myanmar, Indonesia, China, Nepal (3x), India (12x), Kazakstan, Kyrgyzstan, Uzbekistan, and Egypt.

What follows are a few stories from some of those trips.

Ian Bin Soon kisses a Bible Brent gave him after accepting Christ in South Korea in 1997.

VI. Ian Bin Soon – Seoul, South Korea (1997)

"But He gives a greater grace. Therefore it says, 'God is opposed to the proud, but gives grace to the humble.' "
James 4:6

The Korean Peninsula was mainly an agricultural area until after the Korean war. Then South Korea emerged as an industrial and economic center of trade and commerce. This was largely influenced by Christian missionaries and democratic values embraced by the government and its citizens. Contrast this with North Korea's experiment in communism and military dictatorships, which has left millions starving and detractors tortured and imprisoned.

Our team visited the Demilitarized Zone which was a stark dividing line between south and north, good and evil, prosperity and despair. Each day we went into the business suburbs of Seoul, sharing the Gospel and passing out tracks in the Korean language. The people were not open to our message, though, as prosperity had brought a comfortable sense of living without the need for worshipping God. In some cases, people spit on us and threw our tracks on the ground.

We were a bit discouraged as a team, but came together in a morning prayer meeting asking God to use us that day. We had a special evening service planned where we were presenting the Gospel, and we wanted to invite as many people as possible. We went out and shared again, and on this day Michelle cried out to God to send her just one person who would receive the Gospel.

We were on the street and saw a young man and approached him. His name was Ian Bin Soon. He told us that that morning he had woken up and said to himself, "I'm going to find God today." We were thrilled that this divine connection occurred, and we invited him to attend the service that evening. He said he would come, so we departed and went back to our meeting place for the service and looked forward to seeing Ian Bin Soon... no pun intended.

Good to his word, Ian came to the church meeting and stood up at the end of service with others to publicly receive the Gospel and dedicate his life to God. We then gave him a Bible, which he kissed, then asked, "What is the significance of a white bird?"

Brent asked him why he asked, and Ian said, "I saw a white bird on Brent's head as he was sharing the message."

Brent told Ian that the bird was a symbol of the Holy Spirit and was amazed that Ian saw this happen. Ian had never read the Bible before in his life.

It was such a blessing, and an answer to Michelle's prayer, that God would send us one person who would receive THE ONE who could take away all his sins and give him a new life forever. Praise the Lord!! In reflecting back on this experience of "finding" Ian Bin Soon, I am reminded of the Parable of the Lost Sheep, which appears in the gospels of Matthew (18:12-14) and Luke (15:3-7). Jesus emphasized in this story that the shepherd left the 99 sheep to find the one that was lost. It shows just how important one sheep is to the Shepherd and one soul is to the Savior. When the one sheep is found, the Shepherd is overjoyed! When ONE soul is saved, ALL of heaven rejoices! Father God is not willing for anyone to perish, so He seeks and saves the lost, one at a time, in a most dedicated and loving way. Oh, thank you Jesus for finding US, and for making us your own!!!

A view of Brent's plane after landing in the just-opened town of Jomsom in the Mustang district of Northern Nepal on the Tibetan border in 1997.

VII. Window of Opportunity (1997 – 2002)

"For the grace of God has appeared,
bringing salvation to all people..."
Titus 2:11

a. Nepal (1998 – 1999)

Michelle and I led a prayer meeting every week at Fairfield Baptist Church where we prayed for the unreached people groups of the world. We did this for over a year, and out of this came an opportunity to go on a mission trip to South Korea to learn more about planting cell churches.

There was one people group that God put on my heart, the Mao, but I had never heard of such a people group and didn't know for sure if such a people group existed. I later encountered not just one group with this name, but three in three different countries: Nepal, India, and China!

God used our time in South Korea to launch our other efforts throughout the 10/40 Window. It began as we were sitting in the balcony of one of the largest churches in South Korea, learning about cell churches, when we met a woman named Ruth Bhandari. She was the wife of Rev. Lok Bhandari, a Nepali pastor who at the time was president of Kathmandu Seminary. Ruth invited us on our first trip to Nepal in 1998.

Among those who went on this trip were my father Richard Knapton and my wife Michelle. We also met Rev. Nandu Gurung, whom I would visit on several more occasions throughout my life.

I was asked to speak at a prayer conference in conjunction with the seminary graduation along with other speakers including Daniel Kim and Mike and Cindy Jacobs. In typical Nepalese culture, the men sat on one side of the room and the women on the other, all sitting on the floor.

I was praying for some of the men in the men's section when a man asked me to pray for his wife in the women's section. He escorted me into the middle of the group of women and introduced me to his wife. As I began to pray for her, she literally started slithering on the floor like a snake and then wrapped herself around both my legs. I became righteously indignant against this demonic force that dared to cause a distraction in the middle of a sacred assembly. I rebuked the evil spirit in Jesus' name, and as it left the woman, she was flung over the women's section and slammed into the wall fifteen feet away.

I had never seen anything like this before. Several of the women on the mission team went over, checked on her, and kept praying for her. She was not only physically okay, but also delivered and set free from bondage! Praise the Lord!! Her pastor-husband was tremendously grateful. That encounter taught me to never underestimate the enemy and to always take authority over the enemy's attacks in the name of Jesus.

I John 4:4b (NKJV)

"… because He who is in you is greater than he who is in the world."

After the conference and graduation, several of our team flew in a tiny twin-engine airplane up to 14,000 ft. to land in Jomsom, Nepal, in the Mustang district on the border of Tibet. This was a dangerous area because of the Maoist rebels from China who were trying to bring communism into Nepal. The district had only opened to outsiders the previous month for the first time in decades due to political unrest between Tibet and China, including the exile of the Dalai Lama to India.

We trekked several miles to a small village where we prayed for a "man of peace," as the Bible says in Luke 10:6, *"If a man of peace is there, your peace will rest on him; but if not, it will return to you."* A man of peace did greet us at the gate of the village and invited us into his home to meet his newborn daughter.

After this we met a young man named Anyang. His father was an alcoholic, having been introduced to drinking by the Peace Corps that had come into the village years earlier to work on community development projects. I told Anyang our team was a different kind of "peace corps." "We represent Jesus, the Prince of Peace, who can transform your life spiritually, and by reading God's word and sharing it with others, He could also transform your community." Anyang was very eager to pray and accept Christ into his heart to get what he termed, "a white heart," a clean heart.

Isaiah 1:18a (NKJV)
"Come now, and let us reason together," "Says the Lord, "Though your sins are like scarlet, they shall be white as snow..."

While this was happening, part of our team was on the other side of the village where they met a man named Tenzing. He also prayed to receive Christ. Later that day, when our team reunited, we were pleasantly surprised and excited to find out that Anyang and Tenzing were best friends! God was forming a small nucleus of a believing community in the midst of an unreached village. We provided them Nepali Bibles and asked the new pastor in Jomsom to follow up and disciple them.

Three years later, I returned to Nepal with a medical team, and we flew back to Jomsom to continue to establish the church there. We set up a clinic and showed the *Jesus* film for the patients waiting to see the doctors. If we were unable to completely treat a sickness or disease, we would invite them to come to our hostel to receive prayer in the evening. Our Scriptural basis for doing this was Luke 10:9 (NKJV), *"And heal the sick there and say to them, 'The kingdom of God has come near to you.'"*

One man came the first evening with a severely deformed and withered arm which he could not move. I remembered him from the clinic and felt compassion toward him. I did not have the faith to pray for his healing, but God inspired one of the nurses on our team, Paula Smith, who was eager to pray for him. Her pastor had preached a sermon about Jesus healing a man with a withered hand the Sunday before she departed on the mission trip. I encouraged Paula to pray for this man while I stood back watching. I was amazed to see the man lift his arm and open his hand above his head as tears of joy began to pour down his face!! Praise the Lord! I immediately felt a sense of remorse for lacking faith to pray for him, but God in His grace provided Paula. I went over to the man and asked through an interpreter, "Do you know who has healed you?"

He said, "Yes," and stated the name of his god. This man had built an altar of stones on the mountain and had prayed to his deity, but to no avail. I immediately told him it wasn't his god who healed him, but it was Jesus Christ of Nazareth. I was shocked to hear the sound of another voice coming through the man yelling at me in anger. I knew it was demonic, and I rebuked it and cast it out in Jesus' name. The demon left, and the man was relieved to be healed and delivered. I led him in a prayer to accept Jesus as his savior and Lord. I don't get too concerned about the order in which God brings people to salvation, I just know that God saves, heals, and delivers.

John 3: 5-8 (NKJV)

"Jesus answered, "Most assuredly, I say to you, unless one is born of water and the Spirit, he cannot enter the kingdom of God. That which is born of the flesh is flesh, and that which is born of the Spirit is spirit. Do not marvel that I say to you, 'You must be born again.' The wind blows where it wishes, and you hear the sound of it, but cannot tell where it comes from and where it goes. So is everyone who is born of the Spirit."

This man then went out into the streets of Jomsom showing everybody his healed arm, and many came to faith in Christ through his healing. I was further amazed to find out this man had damaged his arm when a boulder fell on him while working to build a small runway on the side of the mountain! Praise the Lord for always making a way! God, in His divine providence, had allowed us to come to his village on the very runway he had constructed and where he was injured to then be healed and bring many in his village to the Lord.

I wept uncontrollably as I witnessed God's sovereign plan unfold.

Just a portion of the thousands who stood and responded to an invitation to repent and follow Jesus in Manipur, India.

b. India (1999 - 2000)

On the day before I was taking a mission team to Delhi, India, for two weeks, I received a phone call from Dr. Lorho Pfoze, a medical doctor visiting the U.S. who was from Manipur, India. He called to ask if I could bring a team to Imphal, the capital of Manipur. I told him I was already on my way the next day with a team headed to Delhi. He was overjoyed at the possibility that we might extend our trip to come visit his city as well. To this day I still don't know how he got my phone number!

I was honored at the request, but I had to call each team member immediately and ask if they would be willing to extend their mission trip an extra eight days. Every team member said, "Yes"! So I overnighted a copy of our passports to Dr. Lorho as he would need them to apply for a restricted access permit to visit Imphal. He received our passports the next day and flew back to Manipur the day after that to apply for the permits for our team. At that time, Manipur was restricting foreigners from entry without a permit because of the intense and violent warfare between the Naga and Kuki tribes. Even with a permit, foreigners could only stay within the boundary of the capital city, Imphal.

As background, this tribal fighting began after British colonization. In order to subdue the Naga tribe, the British army hired the Kuki tribe from neighboring Burma as mercenaries and then deeded them the land they occupied as payment for their service in the British army. After the British left India, the Naga tribe began to fight for the return of their land and the Kuki tribes resisted because they had legal documentation to prove the land now belonged to them. The Indian army was present in the state as a peace-keeping force (and enforcers of the permits) but some corrupt officials were actually selling arms and ammunition to both tribes to prolong the conflict and make extra money. This is why it would be unsafe for foreigners like us to travel there, so that is why access was restricted using a permit process.

Our team flew to Delhi as planned, and we ministered on Sunday morning to the believers at Bethel Church pastored by Simon Haqq who I had been introduced to by Dr. Paul Rains. God led us to wash and anoint all of the members' feet with oil. This was a very moving and emotional experience for both the believers and our mission team. We were following the example Jesus gave His disciples as recorded in the book of John 13:5-9 (ESV):

> *Then He poured water into a basin and began to wash the disciples' feet and to wipe them with the towel that was wrapped around Him. He came to Simon Peter, who said to him, "Lord, do You wash my feet?" Jesus answered him, "What I am doing you do not understand now, but afterward you will understand." Peter said to Him, "You shall never wash my feet." Jesus answered him, "If I do not wash you, you have no share with me." Simon Peter said to Him, "Lord, not my feet only but also my hands and my head!"*

The Bethel believers, like Peter, were initially reluctant for foreigners to touch their feet. However, the act of humility and servanthood ministered greatly to them as we shared a special bonding moment together like Jesus and His disciples. Truly, we experienced the ministry of Jesus that day through the Holy Spirit.

After more ministry during the week in various homes, we flew to Imphal and landed at the heavily militarized airport. We met with immigration officials who were holding our restricted access permits. However, in the rush to get them submitted and approved, and a lack of communication once our team was in Delhi and Dr. Lorho was back in Manipur, the start dates on the permits were for the following day. This meant we could not go out of the airport and would have to fly back to Delhi and then fly back to Imphal the next day. This would have been a huge expense and inconvenience.

Dr. Stephen Klinker, an oral surgeon and leader of our medical team, wisely suggested we conduct an onsite dental clinic for all the airport staff and officials, provided we be allowed to enter the capital city that evening to go to our hotel to stay until the following day when our permits became valid. Thankfully, the general in charge agreed with this arrangement and was the first to receive a free dental checkup!

There was another young official who I talked to after he received his checkup who seemed a bit sad, so I asked if there was something bothering him? "Yes," he said, he was a Muslim and had just returned from the Hajj (a pilgrimage) to Mecca, Saudi Arabia.

I asked him, "Did you meet your god there?"

He said, "NO." He went on to say that he had done all the required religious requirements before and after the ceremonies, but none of this gave him a sense of fulfillment.

I then asked him, "Would you like to receive the One true living God in your heart right now?"

He said, "Who is this God you are talking about?"

After hearing about who Jesus is, he prayed with me to have his sins forgiven through Jesus' sacrifice for him. He had such joy in his heart after praying! I knew God was going to use him to witness to his family and many others in the days and years to come.

After we finished the impromptu dental clinic, we were able to clear customs, then met Dr. Lorho and his wife Apinao. They were very excited to see us and explained to us that our restricted access permits had been rejected when they initially submitted them. They prayed and resubmitted them under an appeal process, which went all the way up to the Assistant Chief Secretary of Manipur. Not only did he approve the permits, which normally would only allow us access to the capital city of Imphal, but he extended our access to the entire state of Manipur! This was unprecedented for foreign visitors at that time. Dr. Lorho was very excited to take us to his home village in the very northern region of Manipur. He was, amazingly, from the Mao tribe, the name which was one of the unreached people groups God had told me to pray for years before!

We were also amazed at the look on the military officers at several security checkpoints along the route to his village who were in disbelief that foreigners were traveling along the road in that area. We felt safe with our host, plus the fact that we were not out after dark.

We were able to have dinner one night with the Secretary General of Manipur. We explained to him that we wanted to bring a larger team the next year and conduct medical clinics and open-air meetings in the community soccer field. He was supportive of this plan, so we spent the rest of our time communicating this idea to various church leaders in the area.

A year later, we brought back a larger team, including William Lau, founder of a healing and evangelistic outreach ministry called the Elijah Challenge and a friend named Ann, a community development specialist. The theme of our meetings was "Repent, Turn, and Follow Jesus." We were amazed to see over 5,000 people gather on the soccer field. There were a variety of native tribal dances to welcome our team, ranging from young children to senior adults. As I watched the tribal dances, I was reminded of native American Indian tribes and the similarities of the dances around blazing fires. I have no doubt that the Native American Indian tribes migrated from Southeast Asia across the Alaska land bridge into the North American Continent centuries before this time.

After preaching a simple message about the cross, several thousand people stepped forward and stood in silence for over half an hour as the tangible presence of God manifested and rested on all of us. No one dared to speak, even the young children, in the presence of God. It was truly a holy moment. Afterward, many people said they had felt a tangible presence of a hand on their heads.

There was a young crippled boy whose legs were bent behind him and had no muscles. His legs were like toothpicks. Honestly, I was afraid to pray for him because I thought if he tried to walk, he would collapse and injure his frail legs. God was faithful and not only straightened his legs, but gave him the strength to walk. There was no showmanship or shouting, simply reverence and a sense of awe, experiencing the glory of God in such a healing way.

The first people to confess their sins and accept Christ as their savior were the pastors of the local churches. You need to understand the history of the Mao tribe in order to realize what was happening. A century before, Scottish missionaries William and Elizabeth Pettigrew had journeyed to Manipur to bring the Gospel. The first tribe they encountered in the northern area were vicious headhunters. The Pettigrews immediately departed to the safety of another tribe, the Thangkul. This tribe were not headhunters, and they received the Pettigrews and also willingly received the Gospel when it was proclaimed to them. God's blessing and provision became evident to all the surrounding tribes, including the Mao. The leaders of the Mao tribe adopted Christian rituals in hopes that they would receive similar blessings. However, they had not truly repented and turned from their sin. Although they built churches throughout their villages, they were not true communities of faith and represented only ritual and social gatherings.

Fast forward to the year 2,000 when the entire community not only heard the Gospel but saw and experienced the power of the Gospel in the lives of their leaders and the most needy individuals. Praise God for this work of transformation! To God be the glory!!

Many years after our visit, Dr. Lorho Pfoze ran and was elected as Minister of Parliament where he serves in Delhi, India. He has most recently been coordinating with churches and Christian leaders to battle the COVID epidemic that has ravaged India in 2021.

Two more stories before I leave India, one short and the other a bit longer.

On another visit to Bihar, a young couple, Wilson and Natalie Geisler, were part of our short-term team from Austin and Houston, Texas. Over the years, I had heard a lot of negative criticism about the ineffectiveness and limited impact of such ventures. My experiences had, by God's grace, been different, and this one was no exception, as Wilson sensed on our trip that God was calling him to move to India, learn the local language, and to train national leaders how to plant reproducing churches. He wisely waited until his wife had a similar calling and, together with their children, they made the move and were very effective disciplers and trainers in Bihar and Nepal for over seven years. I learned to ignore negative criticism when it was unfounded or misplaced. Due to a rare disease that afflicted Natalie, the Geislers later moved back to the U.S. and remain in strategic leadership in international missions mobilization for one of the largest global harvest forces on the planet.

On yet another visit, we took a medical doctor from the U.S. who had just initiated a divorce proceeding against his wife. He had asked me before the trip if this would disqualify him from going. He also said his fifteen-year old son was angry with him because of the upcoming divorce, and he wanted the son to come on the trip to spend time discussing and reconciling with him on this major issue affecting them. I prayed and encouraged him to still come, trusting it into God's hands. Knowing this did give me a special prayer burden to pray for a breakthrough in his life or and to ask God for anything I could say to help him in his situation.

The last day of the trip, we had so many patients arriving that this doctor asked me to step in and help him diagnose the patients. We needed two lines instead of one! The first man who sat down in front of me had a pronounced twitching on one side of his entire face. I immediately thought an injection of a pain-numbing medicine from our dental clinic would help him. So I talked to Dr. Klinker to get his assistance. He examined the man and told me that in his professional opinion, the man was not suffering from a physical ailment, but a spiritual one. He felt so strongly about this that he refused to inject the pain-numbing medicine and suggested I pray for him instead.

Although I had prayed for many people many times before, I honestly felt this situation required a medical solution. But I valued the dentist's input and deferred to his recommendation.

I asked the man for permission, then laid one hand on his face and commanded the twitching to stop. I was honestly shocked when it immediately ceased! The man was smiling broadly, and I asked him to sit next to me for a time because I thought the twitching might start back up. But it didn't!

The medical doctor who was going through a divorce saw this miracle, and the next person who sat in front of him was an elderly man who was deaf in both ears. He could not hear or talk to the translator and his speech was very loud and unintelligible, a sign that he had been deaf for quite some time.

So I told the doctor to pray for the man. He prayed, but nothing happened. I then suggested that we both speak into each of his ears at the same time, and we would say, "Ear, be opened, in Jesus' name."

On the count of three, we both spoke into the man's ears. To our utter amazement, the man was able to have a conversation with the interpreter at a lower volume, and the interpreter confirmed the man was hearing and understanding what he was saying. I saw the eyes of the interpreter open wide in astonishment just as the doctor and I were astonished, as there was no communication going on before.

In that moment, the Holy Spirit prompted me to say to the doctor, "If God can use you to pray for this man and see his ears opened, can He not use you to reconcile with your wife?"

The doctor began to weep and told me he would go back to the U.S. and cancel the divorce proceeding. That night, we shared the news with his son and they embraced, reconciled, and the son's joy was overflowing.

The doctor went home and followed through on his promise to cancel the divorce proceeding.

God's healing of the first man whose face was twitching gave us faith to act and believe God could heal the deaf man as well. And that, in turn, gave us grace for the doctor's marriage to be healed. I was going down the wrong path, looking for a medical solution, until God intervened and put us on a different path that led to two men and a family to be healed that day! So again, I marvel at the grace of God and the way He works. Only God could do those things, and only through surrender and obedience to God's purpose, plan, and will was I able to see the hand of God move in a mighty way that day.

All praise and glory to God!

Brent (third from the left) with a team in Myanmar in 1999, including Dr. Steve Klinker (left) and Dr. Karl Vuta (kneeling).

c. Myanmar (2000)

We faced a difficult challenge in bringing a medical team into Myanmar, formerly known as Burma. Although there were fledgling hopes for democracy, led by Ayn Su Chi, the military ran Myanmar as a dictatorship restricting foreigners from sharing the gospel and persecuting national Christian leaders within the country.

I was aware of these challenges and had deep concerns that if we did our traditional open air services in the evening, we or our host Dr. Karl Vuta, would be arrested and put into jail. In my many discussions with him prior to our trip, he emphatically encouraged us to bring our team and shared with me he had already been imprisoned three times and would be willing to go back for the sake of the Gospel. I was amazed and overwhelmed with his sacrificial love for his people and the Lord.

We made a strategy that we would not be in a location more than one day so by the time word spread to the military and they mobilized a response we should be gone from that location. Also, on the weekend, we would tour historic and museum sites because we were guests in the country on tourist visas. Every day we had wonderful experiences interacting with the people who were very hungry to hear the Gospel because they had been restricted from it for so long. On the last day of the trip we were scheduled to fly to Thailand and back to the U.S. late in the afternoon. We originally planned to visit a market near our hotel and do some souvenir shopping, then eat lunch and drive to the airport.

Dr. Vuta called me early in the morning and asked if our team would do a half-day medical clinic and outreach in a new area we had not been to before. Even though we were tired, we felt like God had brought us here to reach as many people as possible, so we all agreed to conduct the half-day clinic.

Dr. Vuta did not travel with us to the new area because he was making transportation arrangements for our departure. When we arrived at the designated location, we started to unpack. But before we could, military and immigration officials arrived and began interrogating me. They demanded our passports, and I honestly replied that we did not have them, but that they were back at the hotel in a safe behind the reception desk. The officials were angry with us for what we were doing and demanded that we pack up and drive back to the hotel so they could confiscate our passports. With no other alternative, we complied and journeyed back to the hotel. Thankfully, I had invested in long-range, two-way radio transmitters and was able to contact Dr. Vuta and explain our dilemma. God gave me the grace to devise a plan which I communicated over the radio.

Step 1. Our team along with Dr. Vuta synchronized our watches as we drove back.

Step 2. As soon as we arrived at the hotel, we collected and distributed everyone's passport to each team member and sent them off to the market to scatter and shop for souvenirs for one hour. I gave my passport to Dr. Klinker so that I would not have to give it to the immigration official who I would meet at the hotel while everyone else was shopping.

Step 3. After shopping, the team would return to the back of the hotel where Dr. Vuta would have already loaded their luggage into the vans. We would then depart for the airport.

Step 4. I would remain at the hotel and meet the immigration officials, stalling them until the team returned and departed safely to the airport without me.

Step 5. We would pray fervently and trust God for a way in which I could join the team before being detained and taken to a local police station.

Thankfully, traffic was very bad and the immigration officials showed up at the hotel 30 minutes after we arrived. This reduced the amount of time I had to engage with them before making my escape. When the officials arrived and demanded our passports, I told them honestly that our team had taken them and gone shopping to invest money in the local economy. I was adamant that we were lawful guests in their country and did not appreciate being treated in a demeaning manner. The officials talked among themselves trying to figure out what they were going to do with me since they did not obtain our passports.

I kept praying for God to provide a way out of this escalating saga. The one-hour, agreed-upon rendezvous time coincided with the head official stepping outside of the hotel lobby into the street to smoke a cigarette while he was waiting for another military official to come and arrest me for further questioning. I then asked the remaining official if I could use the restroom, and he agreed. I quickly made my way to the back of the hotel where the team was relieved to see me as much as I was relieved to see them! We then got in the van and sped off to the airport. We checked our luggage and cleared security and customs at the airport and were sitting in the waiting area to be called to board our flight. I was alarmed to see a military escort enter the airport where we were seated. However, they stopped and called out the name of a local person who stood up, identified himself, and was immediately handcuffed and escorted out of the airport.

I have never been more relieved in my life to get on an airplane than I was that day. As I sat in my seat, I thanked the Lord for making a way of escape... and I asked the Lord to never send me back there again. This was my thought in the emotion of the moment. If the Lord were to send me back again, I would gladly say, "Yes."

Acts 9:23-25 (ESV)

"When many days had passed, the Jews plotted to kill him, but their plot became known to Saul. They were watching the gates day and night in order to kill him, but his disciples took him by night and let him down through an opening in the wall, lowering him in a basket."

In the years since that trip, I have often wondered what would have happened if I had been detained and arrested and put in jail, but God's grace was sufficient and He provided a plan and a way of escape, for which I am eternally grateful.

Christians around the world need to pray for Myanmar in the aftermath of the military coup that occurred on February 1, 2021. Democratic protestors are being killed in the streets and thousands of people are fleeing to India and living in refugee camps. We are seeking to open LIVE Schools in the camps so young leaders can be trained and equipped to return to Myanmar when the political situation stabilizes.

A view from the pulpit looking out to a completely full crowd of 5,000 Egyptians who had gathered to hear the Gospel in El-Mina, Egypt, in 2002.

d. Egypt (2002)

In the fall of 2001, I was contacted by my good friend William Lau (founder of The Elijah Challenge), and we joined together to plan an outreach in El-Mina, Egypt, seven hours south of Cairo. Because of the crowds expected, the Lord led us to design and build a tent made of hundreds of afghan carpets, which we strung together to form the four walls and roof. We could roll up the carpets to allow air to flow through the tent when needed.

In anticipation that we would have to keep the carpets unrolled due to wind, sand or nightfall, I bought 100 ceiling fans and we installed ten rows of ten fans in each row. We also rented 5,000 chairs and planned for four consecutive nights of outreach. I honestly struggled with my faith in how God would mobilize 5,000 people by even the last day of the meetings, because typically a small crowd comes the first day, but grows as word of mouth lets more people know about the meetings.

God, however, spoke very clearly to me and said He would bring 20,000 people! 5,000 *different* people each day! This changed our strategy in that we had to mail out invitations for people to attend on only one day. Our volunteers mailed out 5,000 invitations for Monday only, Tuesday only, Wednesday only, and Thursday only. This totaled 20,000 invitations.

I had my doubts, but if we had a twenty percent response rate, and each household brought an average of five people, we would have 5,000 each night. Again, to my utter amazement, God brought *exactly* 5,000 people each of the four nights! There were *no* empty seats and *no one* was standing without a seat! I'm an engineer and focus on very specific numbers, and I am not exaggerating in any way! It was a miracle, as can be seen in the photos we took of the crowds under the tent.

I hired the Egyptian army to provide security around the tent and individual bodyguards for each team member, as the 9-11 terrorist attack in NYC had occurred just ten months before this outreach and four of the terrorists were from Cairo, Egypt.

We had permission from the mayor of El-Minia, who was not a believer, to hold the meetings. He attended some of the meetings and his son attended every day. His son ended up praying to receive Jesus Christ as his savior before the end of the outreach.

The first day, Monday, of our medical clinic, an elderly woman began screaming. I rushed over to see what all the commotion was about and began speaking to her son, who was bilingual, because she could only speak Arabic. Her son told me she had been blind in her left eye for five years and God healed her in that very moment. The eye doctor on our team who prayed for her came from a very conservative, cessationist church in Houston, but I had trained him before coming on the trip to lay hands on a patient, with permission, and command healing according to Jesus' instructions in Luke 9:1-2 and 10:1, 9 (ESV):

"And He called the twelve together and gave them power and authority over all demons and to cure diseases, and He sent them out to proclaim the kingdom of God and to heal."

"After this the Lord appointed seventy-two others and sent them on ahead of him, two by two, into every town and place where He himself was about to go... 'Heal the sick in it and say to them, 'The kingdom of God has come near to you.' "

This kind of bold prayer doesn't always result in instantaneous healing, but in this case, it did.

I was in awe and amazement and wanted to document this miracle, so I rented a car and asked the woman's son to take her to her village, see her eye doctor, and bring back a report. This woman and her son had walked 30 kilometers to attend the clinic and meeting that night because they had no car of their own. The eye doctor wrote on her report that she had 20/20 vision (but that he didn't believe God had healed her as she was insisting).

I shared the report with the Presbyterian leaders of the outreach, and they were amazed. Instead of just having an invitation for repentance and salvation after the service, they authorized us to also pray for anyone who was sick. God graciously healed many of various types of illnesses.

Luke 4:40 and 6:19 (ESV)

"Now when the sun was setting, all those who had any who were sick with various diseases brought them to Him, and He laid His hands on every one of them and healed them."

"And all the crowd sought to touch Him, for power came out from Him and healed them all."

Ashraf Kamel, the Egyptian Director of Campus Crusade for Christ, wrote a letter (which follows) documenting all the details of the outreach, including 10,000 people standing to repent and receive Christ and hundreds healed as William Lau spoke and our team prayed over those in need.

November 10, 2002

Dear Brother Brent,

I want to thank you so much for your love, kindness and effort. I can tell you that you are a "Man of God." Really I saw your big heart with practical actions not by words. I saw your wisdom, mind and calm. I'll not forget those days when God makes a great change in my life and my staff. I want to tell you more and more about the results of those days...

1. I want to thank you very much for your love. You and your team are a wonderful team. We saw and touched Jesus through the team. We saw and touched Jesus through your prayers, acts, behaviors, words and ministry. You sacrificed your time, money, effort and all your life to come to minister to people you didn't know at all, really this is Jesus' love.

2. Maybe you came with your team just for evangelistic parties but really you did more:

a. You changed our attitude about healing. You put in a new one. God used you to change our mind and thought. It was the first time in El -Minia to have a conference about healing. All the leaders and the pastors were affected with that conference.

b. You joined two big church communities together... the members of Campus Crusade in El-Minia with the members of the evangelical church in Saft El Laben, especially the leaders have become close friends.

c. You encouraged about 100 staff leaders and students in those days by working together.

d. I confess that every staff member has at least one situation which makes him weep with tears.

e. It's the first time to see 20,000 have very bad illness and circumstances and illness in four days. We saw how much Satan had done and the great challenge to defeat him through healing people and casting out these illness and trouble.

3. *My general observation of this campaign is wonderful.*

a. It was the first time in El-Minia but also in Egypt to have an event like this where we have 20,000 people in four days and two meetings everyday. That is an historical event in Egypt. We make a big tent which takes 5,000 chairs that the attendants of 5,000 daily from different districts, towns, different levels in teaching, and in living.

b. We make about five clinics for different cases for men and women, old and children, all kinds of people. We had about 1,500 cases through those days that took medicine, glasses and other things for free.

c. The seminar about healing encounters encouraged the leaders and pastors to practice healing in their churches. It was a very new teaching in our churches.

4. *My observation and impact of the campaign on the work of the gospel in El-Minia. I can say that it was more than we expected. As my town is not large and I know many people so after the events many people in the streets asked me about spiritual matters and to make the event again.*

5. *About miracles: To see the blind and God open their eyes and to see a lame man walk, it makes many things and our people in El-Minia some encouraged by their healing, others take a new step in faith, others asking God to have this power.*

6. *After you go back to your home many cases came to our office saying they were healed but they could not stand and share their testimony because it was so crowded. Another came with her child and he was four years old. He had a bad disease in his chest and he was completely cured. An old man could not move, his son's wife came to our office to explain how God healed him in those days.*

7. *Let me share some statistics;*

a. About 20,000 people attended these meetings.

b. About 10,000 people accepted Jesus as their savior.

c. About 1,500 were treated in clinics.

8. Let me say I myself have changed in my life, faith and attitude which makes me lead my staff in the office with a new power, new view and new attitude.

9. The last miracle in spite of all these new attitudes, new concepts, new healing is that we didn't face any attack but people love us and appreciate us.

I also want to thank you for the computer. Really it was a great blessing from God through you. It helps me so much in my ministry. I began to make many things in it. Maybe I'll be in the USA in May. Pray for me and may God arrange this journey and may God use me in ministry with the Arab people there and I hope to see you in that time. Of course we will be in touch through the next months and may we arrange to visit you or your church to encourage each other. Don't forget to pray for me and my family and my ministry. God bless you.

Yours,

Ashraf Kamel

Campus Crusade for Christ Director, Upper Egypt El-Minia

As I often reflect on the astonishing outpouring of grace we all witnessed that week, I am reminded of two Old Testament passages:

Isaiah 19:21-22 (ESV)

"And the Lord will make Himself known to the Egyptians, and the Egyptians will know the Lord in that day and worship with sacrifice and offering, and they will make vows to the Lord and will perform them. And the Lord will strike Egypt, striking and healing, and they will return to the Lord, and He will listen to their pleas for mercy and heal them."

Joel 2:28-30 (ESV)

"And it shall come to pass afterward, that I will pour out my Spirit on all flesh; your sons and your daughters shall prophesy, your *old men shall dream dreams and your young men shall see visions. Even on the make and female servants in those days I will pour out my Spirit. And I will show wonders in the heavens and on the earth, blood and fire and columns of smoke."*

Brent and Michelle and their four sons: (left to right) Erik, Luke, Brock, and Michael, July, 2019.

VIII. Family & Brothers Helping Others (2002 – 2019)

"For of His fullness we have all received, and grace upon grace."
John 1:16

After returning from the incredible outreach in Egypt, we set up a special banquet to share the testimonies at our home church, Calvary Community Church pastored by Dr. Steve Meeks and Jeff McGee. In the middle of the presentation, God spoke to my heart and said, **"I did not call you to sacrifice your marriage on the altar of ministry."**

I was once again shocked at the Lord's message and timing because I was so excited to start planning and executing other outreaches in the Middle East, but God was telling me to stop doing mission work completely? I had labored for seven years to get to this point and felt like I was just coming into my element and would impact the lives of several other people on our staff if I stepped down so abruptly.

Like in times before, I clearly knew when God spoke to me and there was no wavering or doubt that I had to obey. I shared this message with our staff and they wholeheartedly supported me and encouraged me by saying they would find another ministry for which to use their talents and abilities to serve the Lord. This was not an easy transition, but God was gracious, as always, and provided a job for me as a project manager in the oil and gas industry.

There were no apparent issues in our marriage, but God knew that if I continued to travel and do trips abroad, our marriage would suffer so He moved me in an entirely different direction. This was a huge blessing because I was now able to focus my attention on being closer to Michelle and raising our sons by being present for their activities and watching their development.

A friend of mine, Brian Blanchard, said to me a very encouraging phrase that I will never forget: "You can take the man out of the mission field, but you can never take the mission field out of the man." This perspective helped me refocus my commitment and energy towards ministering to my family, but I also kept a heart for missions through prayer and financial support. I wasn't sure if I would travel and minister overseas again, but I had to trust God that I was obeying His will and not my own. Over the next several years we had three more sons, Erik, Michael, and Brock, and we had the opportunity to go on some special vacations to Hawaii, the Bahamas, Colorado, Montana, and Washington DC.

God knew I needed an outlet for the ministry call He had on my life, so He provided a small group of men called, "Brothers Helping Others," where I could still pray and help others in ministry. The men in this group are or have been the late Richard Knapton, Rick Sims, Richard Dennis, Gary Frick, Ray Baptista, David Walters, Blake LaGrone, Pat Cook, Mike Watkins, John Prill, and Rogers Schupp. They have ministered back to me and we have been meeting weekly and studying the different books of the Bible for the past thirteen years.

Our format is simple. We meet weekly and study and discuss chapter by chapter until we finish a book, then we meet for breakfast and fellowship and confirm the next book study to start the following week.

In each meeting we all contribute a small offering that gets deposited in Prosperity Bank, the place we have been meeting in the same conference room since 2008. We close our time each week in prayer for one another. There is no designated leader of the group; we all take turns facilitating the discussion on whichever book we study.

As God leads, different ones of us will bring up a need we are aware of and will take the money collected during the preceding months and use it to meet a need. We have sent folks on mission trips, given to international Christian leaders reaching the lost in their communities, helped people with expensive surgeries, and repaired damaged homes. The list goes on. We also invite our spouses to join us for a special Christmas gathering in a home or restaurant each year, and this has further brought us together over the years.

I highly recommend you find a similar group in your area or start one yourself. We all attend different churches in our area which adds to the diversity and richness of our perspectives and discussions.

In addition to fellowshipping with Brothers Helping Others, God has used me to lead Life groups for men at my home church, Christ Family Church, pastored by Paul Russell and his wife Delia. I am also connected to the men's ministry of International Bible Church in Stafford, Texas, led by Rogie George.

Psalms 133:1, 2a, 3b (ESV)

"Behold, how good and pleasant it is when brothers dwell in unity. It is like the precious oil on the head, running down the beard... For there the Lord has commanded the blessing, life forevermore."

A typical Friday morning breakfast at the weekly meeting of "Brothers Helping Others," a group Brent helped organize to minister to one another and those God put on their hearts. This picture includes Richard Dennis, Rich Knapton, Eric Senior, Rick Sims, Tom Dusin, and Gary Frick.

Brent speaking in 2020 in Delhi, India, at the World Mission Centre conference, "Running with Horses."

IX. Assurance – World Mission Centre (2019)

"And the Word became flesh, and dwelt among us; and we saw His glory, glory as of the only Son from the Father, full of grace and truth."
John 1:14

After sixteen years of not hearing a single word from the Lord about my missionary calling, I was shocked and astounded to experience a breakthrough moment when God spoke four profound words to me which would lead to yet another waterfall in my life:

A ccelerated
C ross-cultural
T raining
S eminars

I had no idea what this meant and began to pray and share with close friends in hopes they might have some insight to share with me. One of my best and dearest friends and ministry colleagues over 30 years is Eric Elder. He immediately responded that ACTS sounded a lot like the LIVE School video training program that World Mission Centre (WMC) had created to train national leaders in over 96 nations of the world in fourteen major languages.

Eric soon introduced me to Richard "Dick" Teed, who is on staff with WMC, and who invited me to travel to Columbia, South Carolina, to meet the organization's U.S. directors, William and Shirley Crew. WMC was started by William's father Willie with his wife Lydia in South Africa over 30 years ago.

Coincidentally, it was quite a shock to hear the news that Jacobs decided to sell its downstream oil & gas division to a rival company Worley Parsons. This involved 25,000 employees being acquired by a company with 30,000 employees. Although technically it was an acquisition, in reality it was the merger of two equivalent-sized entities. The leadership of Worley Parsons initiated a reorganization process that involved key leaders interviewing for new positions in the newly created company called Worley.

I was given the opportunity to interview for the position of Director of Project Management, and my interview was scheduled with the vice president of Operations. I drove over to the building and sat in a parking lot and prayed for an hour before the interview.

As I was praying, a car pulled up beside me and parked. I noticed the brand name on the front of the car's tire was "Assurance." This was not a common tire name to me, such as Michelin or Firestone, so it caught my attention. I took a picture of it to remember how God was communicating to me, giving me His assurance that He was with me.

At the last minute, the interview was postponed to the following week, so I ended up driving to my bank to withdraw some money for the weekend trip Michelle and I were making to visit the U.S. office of World Mission Centre in Columbia, South Carolina.

As I was walking toward the bank door, the Lord prompted me to go talk to a man who was in his pickup truck on his cell phone in the parking lot. I didn't want to interrupt his cell phone call, but the Lord prompted me again even stronger that I needed to go immediately and talk to him. I did interrupt his phone call as he asked me, "What can I do for you?"

I said, "Nothing, God has sent me to you. What can I do for you?"

He quickly got off his call and told me his wife had just died after a long battle with cancer. I asked what kind of cancer, and he said pelvic cancer, which my mother had just been diagnosed with and is not a very common form of cancer in general.

He then showed me pictures of his late wife and one incredible photo of the light reflecting off the building behind the hospital room where his wife had stayed, which looked just like an angelic figure. He forwarded me the picture and I sent it to my mother along with the story of meeting David Vasquez. The photo provided a great deal of inspiration and comfort to my mom, and the conversation provided more confirmation to me that God was prompting me to keep reaching out to others.

Soon I was on my way to Columbia, South Carolina, to visit World Mission Centre for the first time. Getting off the plane in Columbia, I saw the word Assurance once again. I took another picture as I knew God was again speaking to me.

When I got back from South Carolina, I was offered and accepted the director position, and in a follow-up training seminar, I saw the word assurance once again in a presentation. The name of the new department was called "Assurance"! I took another picture, knowing that

God was speaking to me of His assurance for a third time in less than a week.

I felt called to be part of the transition, but also felt called more and more into full-time missions.

So in July, 2019, I traveled to Johannesburg, South Africa, for the World Mission Centre's 30th Anniversary celebration conference. This was a special time to meet and get to know the international leadership team members and their families. We also were able to meet with key national leaders from India and confirm plans for the Running with Horses conference in Delhi for over 300 national leaders from across fifteen north India states, as well as Nepal and Bhutan. We also conducted three days of LIVE School Facilitator training for eighteen key leaders across north India, and we distributed 200 LIVE School units, which was a blessing because just two days after the conclusion of our training and return home, India was completely shut down to avoid first wave of COVID. Our India team is led by WMC Founder Willie Crew and consists of myself, Ivor and Hillary Temlett, LeeAnne Reddy, and Richard Teed.

As many new LIVE Schools have opened during the pandemic in northeast India under the leadership of Rev. Nandu Gurung, Rev. Thungdemo Lotha, and Rev. Satish Chettri, we realized that it was imperative to purchase battery powered projectors to enable social distancing for the students as they watched the videos on a wall or screen rather than huddled around a small TV. Before, they had to rely on very intermittent electric power, which would previously cause long delays waiting for power to come back on. With the battery powered projectors, this problem was eliminated and batteries could be recharged each night when power demand was very low. I want to convey my sincere thankfulness for donations made by Matt and

Rike Bowman, owners of Thrive Internet Marketing, and my brother Kurt Knapton and his wife Martha Lu as they were instrumental in getting several projectors to our Facilitators so schools could keep running!

In November of 2020, I was released from Worley and began the support-raising process to join World Mission Centre on a full-time basis as Ambassador for India.

An image Brent saw in his heart and spirit regarding God's grace being poured out as spiritual provision to unreached peoples across the earth.

X. The Vision (Dec. 23rd, 2019)

"After you have suffered for a little while, the God of all grace, who called you to His eternal glory in Christ, will Himself perfect, confirm, strengthen, and establish you."
I Peter 5:10

Michelle and I were praying on the morning of December 23rd, 2019 when the Lord clearly spoke again to me and said, **"Courts and Fields and Courses."** I immediately thought of basketball courts and football fields and golf courses because I am a conditioned sports fan, saved by God's infinite grace! But the Lord instantly showed me He was speaking of His Heavenly Courts and His Harvest Fields and LIVE School Courses!

In my heart and spirit I saw God opening the floor of His Heavenly Courts and releasing parachutes of people and provisions and LIVE School units over the Harvest Fields of unreached peoples across the earth. It was analogous to paratroopers and supplies being dropped to ground troops strategically stationed behind enemy lines in a time of war. I decided to ponder this for a while and look to God's word to confirm…

Malachi 3:10-12 (ESV)
"Bring the whole tithe into the storehouse, so that there may be food in My house, and test Me now in this, says the Lord of Hosts, if I will not open for you the WINDOWS of heaven and pour out for you a blessing until it overflows. Then I will rebuke the devourer

for you, so that it will not destroy the fruits of the ground, nor will your vine in the FIELD cast its grapes, says the Lord of Hosts."

2 Chronicles 16:9 (ESV)

"For the eyes of the Lord run to and fro throughout the whole earth, to give strong support to those whose heart is blameless."

The light of God's truth and revelation are openly received in the place of grace. The more we struggle on our own, pushing our sin up the mountain of pride and self-effort, the darker the shadows grow and the greater the weight of our sin. Through confession and repentance, we return to stand under His waterfall of grace.

XI. Beyond Elementary Teachings

"Therefore leaving the elementary teaching about Christ, let us press on to maturity, not laying again a foundation of repentance from dead works and of faith toward God"
Hebrews 6:1

God wants us to be mature in our living and thinking. I've included below some areas where God has helped me understand His Word.

This is especially true in the following areas.

a. Mercy and Grace

Mercy is when God withholds discipline (or in the case of non-believers and nations, judgement) that is deserved.

Grace is when God gives us gifts we do *not* deserve.

Mercy covers our sin and does not count our trespasses against us (2 Corinthians 5:19).

Grace pours power into our lives to resist temptation, overcome evil and injustice, and fulfill God's will.

II Timothy 1:8-10 (ESV)
"Therefore do not be ashamed of the testimony about our Lord, nor of me His prisoner, but share in suffering for the gospel by the

power of God, who saved us and called us to a holy calling, not because of our works but because of His own purpose and grace, which He gave us in Christ Jesus before the ages began, and which now has been manifested through the appearing of our Savior Christ Jesus, who abolished death and brought life and immortality to light through the gospel."

In my own words: "The place of grace is beholding God's face" (see 2 Corinthians 4:6), and "Go to the throne before you pick up the phone" (see Hebrews 4:16).

b. Confession and Forgiveness

The Bible is clear on these two topics. It is extremely important that we both confess our sin and forgive others who sin against us.

1 John 1:8-9 (ESV)
"If we say we have no sin, we deceive ourselves, and the truth is not in us. If we confess our sins, He is faithful and just to forgive us and cleanse us from all unrighteousness."

James 5:16 (ESV)
"Therefore, confess your sins to one another, that you may be healed. The prayer of a righteous person has great power as it is working."

This may be one of the least practiced verses in the Bible. Our pride tends to keep us from confessing our sins at all, and the fear of judgment or gossip from another believer or group of believers tends to be immobilizing. We need to reach the place of unconditional love and "stringless" forgiveness. What do I mean by "string-less"? I mean "no strings attached!" In other words, I reckon myself as having been forgiven by Christ, so who am I to hold an offense or grudge against someone else? There are many key verses on this topic to help anyone struggling in this area of unforgiveness (see Matthew 18:23-35, Ephesians 4:32, and Colossians 3:13).

c. Healing and Deliverance

I have witnessed many valid and verifiable accounts of healing and deliverance both in the context of out-reach to non-believers as well as to Christians within the Church. I have already mentioned several cases in the preceding chapters of the former, so I will just emphasize again the Scriptural context for this as found in Luke chapters 9 and 10 and in many instances in the book of Acts (Acts 3:6-7, 9:34, 9:40, 14:3, 14:10, 19:12).

We see that in the context of sharing the gospel to the lost, we can rely on the authority Jesus has delegated to us to command sickness and demonic forces to leave. And within God's sovereign will, oftentimes people are healed and delivered quite quickly. Other times the work of God is progressive and takes a longer period of time, some-times hours or even days. On other occasions, I have ex-perienced or witnessed that healing or deliverance did not occur, and I can only relinquish this to the sovereignty of God and not self-defensively blame a lack of "faith" on anyone's part. One does not need to have the spiritual gift of healing (I Corinthians 12:9) to be used by God to command healing when a non-believer is sick, and that person has either given permission when asked by you or they themselves have requested prayer for healing. God is quite able to heal anyone at anytime if He has, by His grace, led you to command healing as Jesus and his disciples did.

A careful study of the Gospels reveals that Jesus spent His early mornings in prayer with His Heavenly Father (Luke 5:16), then most of His afternoons commanding the sick to be healed or the demon possessed to be delivered. He also preached and taught and fed the hungry, but a significant portion of His ministry was freeing people out from under the yoke of slavery to sin and satan (see Acts 13:38-39). Because He had already prayed to His Heavenly Father (and knew what to expect in advance) John says ...

John 5:19-20 (ESV)

"...Truly, truly I say to you, the Son can do nothing of His own accord, but only what He sees the Father doing; for whatever the Father does, that the Son does likewise. For the Father loves the Son and shows Him all that He himself is doing. And greater works than these will He show Him, so that you may marvel."

Jesus therefore commanded healing and deliverance when He encountered people in bondage or in pain. He did not formally pray for them, rather He commanded OVER them.

John 14:12 (ESV)

"Truly, truly, I say to you, whoever believes in Me will also do the works that I do; and greater works than these will he do, because I am going to the Father."

Question: When is the last time you marveled at something God did, either in your life or through you to minister to someone else? If it has been a while, perhaps spending some time alone with God in the early morning hours of the day will lead to the Father showing you something He plans to do through you for His glory but you get to partake in it because He loves you!

Jesus said to Martha:

Luke 10:42 (ESV)
"but one thing is necessary, Mary has chosen the good portion, which will not be taken away from her."

Mary had chosen to sit at Jesus' feet and listen to Him. Martha had chosen to be busy and worry about serving Him. What do you suppose the Lord wants? How about sitting quietly in His presence, then go do what He shows you to do? Don't you think this will be better than burning out doing things you want to do for Him instead of the works He wants to do through you? Martha sought to impress Jesus, but Mary sought Jesus to receive from Him.

God loves you enough to not only want a relationship with you but to work through you to accomplish His will. God will give you the grace and strength and power to accomplish His will after you step out in faith and love and obedience. Pray first, wait second and act third. Acting first without waiting and then praying in desperation is not the way to go!

Some people are reluctant to command healing or deliverance because they have witnessed charlatans who have made a show or mockery of such ministry. Be encouraged that a counterfeit only testifies to the genuine reality. Counterfeits and charlatans should be exposed for the false teachers they are, but do not let the fact that some have gone astray stop you from acting. And don't let criticism or persecution stop you either. If Jesus was maligned for healing the sick and spending time with sinners, we should expect no less, and in fact rejoice, that we are undergoing such trials for His glory.

There are many Scripture verses about deliverance in the New Testament. Matthew 10:1 states that Jesus called his "... *twelve disciples and gave them authority over unclean spirits, to cast them out ...*" We often see Jesus exercising authority over a demon or legions of demons possessing individuals (see Mark 1:25, Luke 4:35, Mark 5:8-13, Mark 9:20-27). We also see the Disciples casting out demons in Luke 10 and in the book of Acts (see Acts 5:16, Acts 16:18, Acts 19:12).

Now let me address the second context of praying for Christians in the church. James chapter 5 gives church leaders and members very specific and simple instructions what to do if someone is sick and needs healing prayer.

James 5:14-15 (ESV)

"Is anyone among you sick? Let him call for the elders of the church, and let them pray over him, anointing him with oil in the name of the Lord, and the prayer of faith will save the one who is sick, and the Lord will raise him up. and if he has committed sins, he will be forgiven."

The process is quite simple, but in all my years of attending various churches, I cannot remember when this was done according to these simple instructions. Some churches had a prayer chain where a request was called into the church secretary and it was posted on some sort of social media platform and members of the church prayed. Other churches sent the senior pastor to the hospital once a month to pray for any church members who may be admitted there. Other churches conducted healing services where an anointed guest speaker would ask sick people to come forward, and he would lay his hands on their heads and declare people healed on the spot. I am sure there are other forms of healing prayer, and some churches that follow James 5:14-15 to the letter, I just happened not to be a member of those churches at the time.

Notice that James also associates sickness with forgiveness of sin. Not always, but in some situations, sickness can be the direct result of sin in the life of the believer. Believers can receive physical as well as spiritual healing from elders who anoint and pray over them. Also notice and do not overlook the word "over." James is not saying to pray "for" the sick person but rather to pray "over" them while anointing with oil. This is significant in that the elder is commanding healing to take place using the authority given him through his appointment into an elder role, taking authority "over" what should not be allowed in the life of the sick person and binding what is already bound in heaven and loosing what is already permitted in heaven is key to see the sick person healed.

Matthew 16: 18b-19 (ESV)

"...I will build My church, and the gates of hell shall not prevail against it. I will give you the keys of the kingdom of heaven, and whatever you bind on earth shall be bound in heaven, and whatever you loose on earth shall be loosed in heaven."

It is also important to remember the exhortation James provides in the next verse:

James 5:16 (ESV)

"Therefore, confess your sins to one another and pray for one another, that you may be healed. The prayer of a righteous person has great power as it is working."

When we are in right standing with God through the blood of Christ, which cleanses us from *our* sin, we can pray for others and expect God's power to be released to accomplish His purpose in the life of a fellow believer. Don't forget the confession part before praying. This reconciles us to God and one another and restores the fellowship that sin may have hindered. It also removes any place the enemy may be taking advantage of to cause sickness or disease. Not all illnesses are directly caused by the presence of an evil spirit, but even if the sickness is a disorder of natural origin attributed to the curse placed on this world when humanity fell, prayer is the means of seeing God manifest His power and bring restoration, wholeness, and healing to the praise of His holy name.

d. Power and Glory

God's power and glory are fascinating to me. These attributes of God reveal His omnipotence like no others. Rather than write out explanations and examples of these two final categories, I would rather list two columns of Scripture verses, one for power and the other for glory and let the words of God speak for themselves.

Power verses	Glory verses
God is my strength and power, and He makes my way perfect. 2 Samuel 22:33 (NKJV)	*Moses said, "Please show me Your glory."* Exodus 33:18
So I have looked upon You in the sanctuary, beholding Your power and glory. Psalms 63:2	*The heavens declare the glory of God, and the sky above proclaims His handiwork.* Psalms 19:1
O God, from my youth You have taught me, and I still proclaim Your wondrous deeds. So even to old age and gray hairs, O God, do not forsake me, until I proclaim Your might to another generation, Your power to all those to come. Psalms 71:17-18	*Sing the glory of His name; give to Him glorious praise!* Psalms 66:2

And Jesus returned in the power of the Spirit to Galilee, and a report about him went out through all the surrounding country.

Luke 4:14

But you will receive power when the Holy Spirit has come upon you, and you will be my witnesses in Jerusalem and in all Judea and Samaria, and to the end of the earth."

Acts 1:8

"And now, Lord, look upon their threats and grant to your servants to continue to speak your word with all boldness, while you stretch out your hand to heal, and signs and wonders are performed through the name of your holy servant Jesus."

Acts 4:29-30

For I am not ashamed of the gospel, for it is the power of God for salvation to everyone who believes, to the Jew first and also to the Greek.

Romans 1:16

It is the glory of God to conceal things, but the glory of kings is to search things out.

Proverbs 25:2

For they loved the glory that comes from man more than the glory that comes from God.

John 12:43

For I consider that the sufferings of this present time are not worth comparing with the glory that is to be revealed to us.

Romans 8:18

To Him be glory in the church and in Christ Jesus throughout all generations, forever and ever. Amen.

Ephesians 3:21

If the Spirit of Him who raised Jesus from the dead dwells in you, He who raised Christ Jesus from the dead will also give life to your mortal bodies through His Spirit who dwells in you.

Romans 8:11

For I will not venture to speak of anything except what Christ has accomplished through me to bring the Gentiles to obedience—by word and deed, by the power of signs and wonders, by the power of the Spirit of God —so that from Jerusalem and all the way around to Illyricum I have fulfilled the ministry of the gospel of Christ; and thus I make it my ambition to preach the gospel, not where Christ has already been named, lest I build on someone else's foundation.

Romans 15:18-20

And my speech and my message were not in plausible words of wisdom, but in demonstration of the Spirit and of power, so that your faith might not rest in the wisdom of men but in the power of God.

I Corinthians 2:4-5

And we all, with unveiled face, beholding the glory of the Lord, are being transformed into the same image from one degree of glory to another. For this comes from the Lord who is the Spirit.

II Corinthians 3:18

For this light momentary affliction is preparing for us an eternal weight of glory beyond all comparison.

II Corinthians 4:17

And my God will supply every need of yours according to his riches in glory in Christ Jesus. To our God and Father be glory forever and ever. Amen.

Philippians 4:19-20

That according to the riches of his glory He may grant you to be strengthened with power through His Spirit in your inner being.

Ephesians 3:16

Now to Him who is able to do far more abundantly than all that we ask or think, according to the power at work within us.

Ephesians 3:20

For this I toil, struggling with all His energy that He powerfully works within me.

Colossians 1:29

...because our gospel came to you not only in word, but also in power and in the Holy Spirit and with full conviction. You know what kind of men we proved to be among you for your sake.

I Thessalonians 1:5

...for God gave us a spirit not of fear but of power and love and self-control.

2 Timothy 1:7

To this He called you through our gospel, so that you may obtain the glory of our Lord Jesus Christ.

II Thessalonians 2:14

...waiting for our blessed hope, the appearing of the glory of our great God and Savior Jesus Christ...

Titus 2:13

If you are insulted for the name of Christ, you are blessed, because the Spirit of glory and of God rests upon you.

I Peter 4:14

And after you have suffered a little while, the God of all grace, who has called you to his eternal glory in Christ, will himself restore, confirm, strengthen, and establish you.

I Peter 5:10

"Worthy are you, our Lord and God, to receive glory and honor and power, for You created all things, and by Your will they existed and were created."

Revelation 4:11

An example from nature of the importance of letting God's grace flow through us, rather than just into us with no outlet. The Sea of Galilee stays fresh while the Dead Sea is stagnant.

XII. Conclusion – A Call for Unity and Maturity

Some people believe that God no longer speaks or heals or works miracles today as he did throughout the Bible. But as you read these stories, I hope you'll see that God really does do each of those things!

I would never have planned for 20,000 people to attend an event in Egypt if God hadn't spoken to me to do so. I would never have seen a woman healed of blindness, and confirmed by a medical doctor, after a member of our team prayed a healing prayer over her. I would never have "gone after" that one lost sheep who came to our retreat unless God had prompted me to pray for 30 days for 30 minutes a day for 30 athletes to attend. What God has done in the past, He can still do today! As the Bible says:

Hebrews 13:8 (ESV)
"Jesus Christ is the same yesterday and today and forever."

Some people believe that these gifts don't exist because they have never experienced them or have been taught otherwise. But God has given many gifts to many people for many different purposes. We don't all have to be the same, nor should we be. We are all one body, but we are not all the same. Oneness is not sameness.

Unity is not uniformity. Unity is diversity working collaboratively together.

Perhaps the best and most familiar analogy I can offer on this subject is that of a football team. Each team has an offensive unit, a defensive unit, and a special teams unit. All the players on the team have different positions, skill sets, sizes, body types, and speed and strength characteristics.

The offensive unit is trying to advance the ball into the end zone through the opposing team's defense. This can be done by running or passing with players blocking ahead of the ball to enable positive yardage to be gained, in most cases. All the players respect the differences in each other that enable them to excel at their different positions, all the while running the same play with the same objective in mind. How ridiculous it would be for the offensive line to demand that the quarterback gain 150 additional pounds and block defenders instead of calling the plays and handing or passing the ball to other players on the team. Nothing would happen if all the players were offensive linemen. Likewise, it would be just as ridiculous to have the running back demand that all other offensive players lose weight and join him in the backfield to run the ball with no upfront blockers. He and any other imposter would be tackled behind the line of scrimmage on every play. The offensive unit relies on a variety of differing talent, size, speed, and agility to effectively execute various plays designed always with the common goal of advancing the ball into the end zone to score a touchdown.

The same holds true for the defensive unit. This portion of the overall team is responsible for preventing the opposing team from advancing the ball or scoring points. They, too, are all different in their appearance, each one trained to perform certain tasks unique to the position they occupy on the field.

And the special teams unit are players who kick or punt or return the ball or block for said players. Their role is to transition the ball to the other team or score a field goal or extra point when called upon to do so within strategic locations on the field and moments within the game. Just like the offensive unit, these players have varying size, skill, and speed that makes them effective in their various roles. All cooperate together to get the job done. How narrow-minded it would be for one of them to demand that all the others look like and act like them. I hope and pray that the Body of Christ will begin to learn lessons from a football team and stop criticizing the different leadership and player positions God has put on the team. Pastors and teachers who have a heart for people and truth must not shun or despise the other positions on the team such as apostle (missionary), evangelist, or prophet. These are office gifts that Jesus gives to His Body, the Church according to Ephesians 4:12-14 (ESV):

"[to] equip the saints for the work of ministry, for the building up of the Body of Christ, until we all attain to the unity of the faith and the knowledge of the Son of God, to mature manhood, to the measure of the stature of the fullness of Christ. so that we may no longer be children, tossed to and fro by the waves and carried about by every wind of doctrine, by human cunning, by craftiness in deceitful schemes."

Paul noted to Timothy on two different occasions that God had called him to three different ministry offices: Apostle, Preacher, and Teacher (see 1 Timothy 2:7 and 2 Timothy 1:11). The Lord has called me to proclaim the gospel to the lost and train local pastors to plant churches among the least-reached people groups on the planet. All my life I have been ministered to, discipled by and accountable to pastors in local churches where the Lord has planted Michelle and me. We have a heart to minister to pastors and missionaries who face challenging responsibilities, so the Lord has connected us with Still Waters Renewal ministries to serve on the board of directors supporting this lifeline of counseling and encouragement to those serving in church leadership roles. One of the most obvious and effective tactics employed by satan's legion of principalities, powers, and world forces is to attack Christian leaders through the criticism and false accusations of their very own church members. Granted, in some rare cases, leaders commit unlawful acts that must be exposed and punished, but in many cases, a leader is innocent and forced out of their position over a doctrinal dispute, personality conflict or unforgiven personal offense. How blessed are leaders who serve and minister to the congregation and in turn are respected and prayed for by the members at large.

Today many church leaders are caught up in publicly criticizing one another over minor doctrinal differences and seldom, if ever, personally confront a leader in love privately in order to guide them back to the path if they have strayed away.

Galatians 6:1 (ESV)

"Brothers, if anyone is caught in any transgression, you who are spiritual should restore him in a spirit of gentleness. Keep watch on yourself, lest you too be tempted."

Galatians 5:14-15 (ESV)

"For the whole law if fulled in one word: 'You shall love your neighbor as yourself.' But if you bite and devour one another, watch out that you are not consumed by one another."

Ephesians 4:29 (ESV)

"Let no corrupting talk come out of your mouths, but only such as is good for building up, as fits the occasion, that it may give grace to those who hear."

Let us endeavor to be people of grace, giving the benefit of the doubt and forgiving those who persecute us. Remember and learn from the football players that do not criticize other players publicly. If a leader believes another leader is teaching false doctrine not contained in the Word of God, then it is incumbent on that leader to meet personally and privately with the other leader and share the concern. They may not ever come to fully agree on the interpretation of the doctrinal matter, but they can depart with mutual understanding and respect and resolve not to publicly criticize each other, which accomplishes nothing except to bring reproach upon church leadership which has already suffered through many moral scandals over the years.

Another area of confusion and controversy is arising over the leadership positions in the church. Paul identifies five primary leadership positions that Jesus gives as gifts to the Church in Ephesians 4:11: Apostle, Prophet, Evangelist, Pastor, and Teacher.

God has used many individuals of all types and positions and backgrounds to receive inspired messages which have been recorded as Scripture and translated down through the centuries. Matthew and John are two of Jesus' original twelve disciples turned apostles who are noted as authors of gospel accounts of His life and ministry. The others followed His command to go into all the world and make disciples, baptize, and teach others all they had learned. Peter is used as a source of Mark's gospel, and he does write two letters to believers in Asia (modern-day Turkey). There are nine other apostles identified in the New Testament who did not write Scripture: Matthias, Barnabas, Apollos, Silvanus, Epaphroditus, two unarmed apostles in II Corinthians 8:23, Andronicus, and Junia. So nine of the original apostles and nine other titled apostles did not write any Scripture, but they functioned in the role of an apostle, "one who is sent as an ambassador to proclaim the gospel and establish churches among differing ethne (ethnic groups)." This is my definition for the sake of context and understanding because many streams of the Christian faith have different terminology and definitions of common words in Scripture. Today there are tens of thousands of individuals identified as "missionaries" (the English translation of "apostle" from Latin from Greek). Many of these individuals are being used by God to translate His Word into the native language of the ethne God has called them to reach. The Bible states that apostles and prophets are the foundation of the church (Ephesians 2:20), and God appointed *"first apostles and second prophets..."* (I Corinthians 12:28, ESV). Apostles (missionaries) and prophets are used by God to go into unreached areas and raise up leadership so that evangelists can follow to reap a harvest, and pastors and teachers can follow to disciple the new believers and equip them for ministry, just as different positions on the football team working collaboratively with other leaders to accomplish the common goal of making disciples.

Let me shift to the role of a prophet as named in Ephesians 4:11. Differing from Old Testament prophets, New Testament prophets *"...speak to people for their upbuilding and encouragement and consolation"* (I Corinthians 14:3b, ESV) and to *"...build up the church"* (I Corinthians 14:4b, ESV). Many Christians do not believe apostles or prophets exist in the body of Christ today (and if they do exist, they are labeled "false"). This is unfortunate and based on narrow interpretations of Hebrews 1:1-2 and I Corinthians 13:8,10. God has spoken in Jesus, but continues to speak to the church through Pastors, Teachers, and Prophets (see Paul's admonition to Timothy in I Timothy 1:18 and 4:14).

The spiritual gift of prophecy is clearly authorized in Romans 12:6, I Corinthians 12:10, I Corinthians 14:6 and I Corinthians 14:22b. Prophecy is encouraged by Paul in I Corinthians 14:39, ESV, "*earnestly desire to prophesy,*" and he explicitly tells the church in Thessalonica, "*Do not despise prophesies*" (I Thessalonians 5:20, ESV). Where churches are not quenching the Holy Spirit and allowing individuals to operate in the gift of prophecy, it is critical to follow Paul's admonition found in I Corinthians 14:32, ESV, "*the spirit of the prophets are subject to the prophets.*" In other words, a mature prophet should correct another prophet if a "so-called" word from the Lord is judged not to be in order or not truly from the Lord. The Bible references false prophets (see Jeremiah 7) and warns again them in II Peter 2:1-3, so it is incumbent on the mature leaders with this gift to ensure it is not misused or abused. God has serious ramifications for false prophets and false teachers, but we should not eliminate these offices and gifts from functioning in the church just because there is possibility for error and misuse. For there to be a counterfeit, there must be a real.

Some claim that these gifts have ceased citing I Corinthians 13:8,10, ESV, "*Love never ends. As for prophecies, they will pass away; as for tongues, they will cease; as for knowledge; it will pass away. But when the perfect comes, the partial will pass away.*" Clearly gifts such as knowledge have not passed away. Paul doesn't elaborate specifically on what he means by "*when the perfect comes,*" so many have speculated that "the perfect" means "the Bible" while others believe it means "the return of Christ." I hold to the latter view because of the word "*comes*" after the word "*perfect.*" In my opinion, the Bible as "perfect" would be more accurately described as "completed" and not "comes." On the other hand, Jesus as "perfect" that "comes" to end prophecy, tongues, and knowledge makes more intuitive sense because we will be transfigured in the twinkling of an eye and take upon immortal and glorified bodies, no longer bound by the curse and constraints of this world (see I Corinthians 15:52-54).

Unforgiveness and bitterness stemming from misunderstandings around church leadership will stop the flow of God's grace in our lives quicker than anything. When the water stops falling and the river stops flowing, stagnation and stench are not far behind. I suppose that is why God gave his people the visual illustration of the Jordan river flowing into the Dead Sea which has no outlet, so nothing lives there but salt (dry and thirsty, not wet and vibrant). We must continue to have outlets for the flow of God's grace, like the Sea of Galilee, which has a continual flow of water coming into and going out of it. These outlets can include local outreaches in neighborhoods or mission trips to unreached people groups around the world. Seek to create some new testimonies of grace that will encourage others for generations to come.

One last comment about the nature of a testimony. "Testimonies" cannot be spelled without the words "Test" and "monies." For me, it seems an endeavor has to have some degree of difficulty and also some degree of provision from God or it doesn't qualify in the "Testimonies" category! Let me be empathetically clear, when God provides funds or resources or prospers you in some way, it is not to be consumed selfishly, but rather used to extend and expand His kingdom, not your own. Are we too content these days to just receive from the hand of God and not continually seek His face? True blessings, true prosperity, and true abundance is found at His feet, in His presence, and not from His hand alone. God's Word teaches us that we are blessed to be a blessing. As God said to Abraham:

Genesis 12:2 (ESV)
"And I will make of you a great nation, and I will bless you and make your name great, so that you will be a blessing."

This is the flow God intends. We stop the flow when we cease to bless others and become a means unto ourselves.

I hope you have been inspired and encouraged to spend time seeking God, then to find the nearest waterfall and share God's grace and power with others. Not only will they be blessed, but you will be blessed from the flow as well. Don't let fear stop you or stop the flow from within. Follow Jesus and Flow in the Spirit to the Glory of the Father!

Isaiah 43:19 (ESV)
"Behold, I am doing a new thing; now it springs forth, do you not perceive it? I will make a way in the wilderness and rivers in the dessert."

Brent loves acrostics as a way to remember truths found in God's Word.

Appendix: A-cross-tics

"The grace of the Lord Jesus be with all. Amen."
Revelation 22:21

Below are several acrostics that I have come up with over the years, starting with FLOW!

F aith
L ove
O bedience
W orship

F orsaking
A ll
I
T rust
H im

H olding
O n with
P rayerful
E xpectancy

M aintaining and
E xercising
R ighteous
C ompassionate
Y earnings

W onderful
O ther
R ighteous
S upreme
H oly
I ncarnate
P raiseworthy

P eservering
A lways
T owards
H im

P eace
R eigning
O ver me
V ictoriously
I 'm
D estined to
E xperience a
N everending
C hrist-filled
E ternity

G od's
I ncarnation
F or
T transgressions

G race
I mparted
F or
T imely
S ervice

L iving
I nfinitely
F or
E ternity

T otally
R esting
U nder
S table
T ies

P owerful
U understanding of
R esources
P eople
O pportunities
S trengths and
E nergies

P owerfully
A ctivating my
S ource of
S trength
I
O rchestrate
N ewness

W alking
W ith
J esus
D aily

YaWeh **T** heWay (The cross "T" in the middle)

Heart = He, ear, hear, art (Words in "the heart")

"Ignite the light to shine bright in the night and fight for what's right with all God's might!"

O bedience to the words of Jesus
I ntimacy with Heavenly Father
L ove for people in darkness (Matthew 25:1-13)

The "Fruit of the Spirit" from Galatians 5:22-23:

L avishing
O thers with
V alidation and
E mpathy

J esus'
O ffering for
Y ou

P urposely
E nveloped in
A
C hrist-centered
E nvironment

P repared
A nd
T ested,
I
E xperience
N eglect and
C alamity with
E ndurance

K ingdom
I inheritance
N ow
D emonstrating
N ew
E xpressions of
S elfless
S acrifices

G od's
O mnipotent
O mnipresent
D estiny and
N ever
E nding
S ecure
S alvation

F orsaking
A ll,
I
T ransmit
H is
F orgiveness and
U nconditional
L ove
N ot
E xcuses or
S inful
S elfishness

G od
E nabling
N ew
T hinking, I
L ive
E xpressing
N ever-ending
E mpathy
S ympathy and
S upport

S hooting
E very
L ittle
F ox
-
C hrist
O mnipotently
a**N** d
T otally
R uling
O ver my
L ife

Brent with Pastor and Brother in Christ Simon Haqq in India in 2017. Simon went to be with the Lord on June 1st, 2021.

In Loving Memory of Simon Haqq

Pastor Simon Haqq was head of the Christian Family Association of India and pastored Bethel church in Delhi. He preached in dozens of evangelistic crusades to millions across north India. He loved the Lord, his church, and the lost with a heart of gold.

I had the honor of ministering alongside Simon on twelve different occasions across north India. He walked in great faith, humility, and most of all love. He shared God's love with everyone he met, and you knew that he loved you deeply by the way he listened to you and ministered into your life through his encouraging smile and kind words of wisdom and grace. He will always be my brother in Christ, and I cannot wait to see him again!

Brent and Michelle Knapton, November, 2018.

About the Author

Brent Knapton received Christ as his savior and Lord at an early age and has had a heart for missions since that time. He grew up in the Dallas/Fort Worth area and attended Bedford Methodist Church where he met Michelle.

Brent attended Rice University with a double major in Mechanical Engineering and Religious Studies, and Michelle graduated from University of North Texas with an elementary education degree. They were married in 1990 and have lived in the Houston area for over 30 years. They have raised four sons together.

Brent founded Window of Opportunity which conducted medical clinics and evangelistic outreaches in the 10/40 Window. He worked in the oil and gas industry for various companies including Stone and Webster (Technip), Jacobs, and Worley. He is currently serving as an ambassador for India with the World Missions Centre and Michelle is serving as prayer coordinator for India.

To see more pictures and videos or learn more, visit:

BRENTKNAPTON.COM